30-DAY CHALLENGE

Live Out

God's Amazing Plans

TAMARA S. DOSS

30-DAY CHALLENGE
Live Out God's Amazing Plans
2018 By Tamara Doss
Amazing Life Ministries
www.GodsAmazingPlans.com

ISBN 978-1-7325050-0-1

Published by *Amazing Life Publishing*
Printed in the United States of America

Dedicated to:

This 30-Day Challenge is dedicated to Jesus Christ, my Lord and Savor and my life journey with Him. This book was born out of a conversation with my Heavenly Father through the Spirit of God who asked me to write down all the key principles that He has taught me over the years and to share it with others, so they can advance and live out their God-given amazing plan.

God directed me to Habakkuk 2:2 where he instructed Habakkuk to write it down so others will not stumble. *"And then GOD answered: "Write this. Write what you see. Write it out in big block letters so that it can be read on the run. This vision-message is a witness pointing to what's coming. It aches for the coming—it can hardly wait! And it doesn't lie."*

Thank you, Father, for entrusting me with this journey and allowing me to share it with the world. Thank you for your unconditional love and guidance throughout my life. Thank you for making me beautiful and perfect in your image. Thank you for giving me strength, courage and boldness to be obedient to your will.

I also want to dedicate this book to you, the reader. I thank you for choosing to join me on this 30-Day Challenge and to change your life by spending time in the presence of Jesus daily. I know there are many struggles, questions and obstacles that have prevented you from truly living out your amazing plan and I pray this journey will transform your heart, mind and soul. Jesus is waiting for you and I am confident that if you seek Him, you will find Him.

Acknowledgements:

I want to thank my wonderful husband, Reggie, for your unconditional love and support. Thank you for never allowing me to give up on who I am and what God has called me to do. Thank you for your confidence and belief in me and my personal relationship with Jesus Christ. Your faith in my relationship with God and belief in me drove me to continue this journey and I love you with all my heart. I am blessed by your love and support.

To my amazing three children Ricci, Robbi and Ronni. Thank you for being you and I am so blessed to have you in my life. I am grateful that God entrusted me to be your mommy. God has great favor on your lives and He has an amazing plan for each of you. I pray each of you discover it and bravely live it out in full color.

To my mother, father, brothers and friends, thank you for believing in me and supporting me in my many life endeavors. Your love and belief in me mean so much to me and I could not be who I am without your love and support throughout the years.

To my many mentors, some know who you are, and some don't, thank you for all your wisdom, knowledge and teachings that you have given me over our years of knowing one another.

I want to thank God for giving me the guidance, strength and focus to finish this book. It was only by the power of the Holy Spirit that this book was given and is written. Now I surrender it back to you.

Tamara's 30-DAY CHALLENGE
"Live Out God's Amazing Plans"

I am so excited that you decided to join me on this 30-Day Challenge to discover YOUR amazing plan! I encourage you to use the journal pages included in this book, devoted to this challenge, so you can document all the exciting encouragement, insight and direction the Lord shares with you.

Some of you may not know the voice of God, so the beginning days may be harder for you until you learn to discern His voice from your own or others. But I promise you, that if you seek Him with all your heart, you will find Him, and you will hear His voice. He will speak with you. Listening for His voice takes practice, an open heart, and daily time devoted to conversation with Him. This Challenge will help you develop the skill of listening to Him and learn His voice. I pray discovering His voice will build your confidence and worth which will empower you to walk obediently.

Every day after reading your Challenge, go to **www.GodsAmazingPlans.com**, find the 30-Day Challenge and click the DAY'S CHALLENGE to watch an encouraging video from me which will offer you my perspective on the daily assignment. Read the instructions on your Day's Challenge and follow the assignment. This Challenge is about getting in touch with the power of the Holy Spirit through Jesus Christ and learning to spend time with Him daily, developing the skills of better listening and becoming obedient to His will. This is how we learn to walk on God's path and not our own. This is how we learn to live out God's amazing plans in our lives.

TABLE OF CONTENTS

TABLE OF CONTENTS

CHAPTER	PAGE

30-DAY CHALLENGE

Personal Experiences and Testimonies

EDIE BOS
Corona Friends Church Women's Ministry Leader, Corona CA

One of the reasons I felt compelled to do the 30-Day Challenge: Live out God's Amazing Plans is because I believe in what God is doing in myself and in others. When my friend Tamara asked if anyone was willing to take this challenge to be encouraged, disciplined, and get back on track, or simply support what the Lord had put on her heart, I simply responded with an emphatic, "Yes!" and I accepted the challenge.

God has an 'Amazing Plan' for each one of us. We often stand in our own way of what God wants us to see. When we stay in touch with Him daily and seek Him with all our heart, that's when we can hear Him more clearly and His Holy Spirit will speak to our hearts and our spirit much louder.

This Challenge put me on a short 30-Day journey with the Lord, strategically and with a specific commission. I needed to get back on track to stay connected in such a way as I am facing new challenges in this season. Having been a Christian for more than 45 years, I still find myself continuing to learn more about who God is in my life and what His design is for me. I have walked the path for many years, but God's mercies are new every morning.

The most gratifying thing in my life is choosing to dedicate myself to the Lord and walk in His ways. I encourage everyone reading this to discover who you are in Christ, to know and understand His plan for you, to walk in it, see the ways He smooths out the rough patches, and to know He is with you every step of the way giving you courage, strength, and wisdom to press on.

In doing this Challenge, I was reminded that I am valued by God and that everything I do impacts me and others around me. I was also brought to my knees at times with a grateful heart remembering what the Lord has brought me through. Each day had its own wonderful take away, or giving, into whatever was needed for that day. I am very grateful to the Lord for my friend Tamara as she has put so much time into this project and has prayed for direction to encourage and edify others for the sake of the Kingdom of Heaven. I encourage everyone to take this Challenge; to allow the Lord to invest into you all that you need and desire.

May God Bless You!

LAWANDA MARTINEZ
Cherish Ministries and PEW Water of Life Community Church and Life Builder Seminars, Rancho Cucamonga, CA

I first saw the 30-Day Challenge on my Facebook feed. What drew me to participate was the word "Challenge." I was excited for an actual spiritual journal challenge. See I have a Fitbit and I do weekly challenges with my friend to encourage movement with motivation. We do the Work Week Hustle, the Weekend Warriors and Daily Goal Challenges though our Fitbit, which we encourage and celebrate one another as to hit our goals. When I saw "God's Amazing Plans 30-Day Challenge" it was appealing to me to do a spiritual challenge especially since our fall bible study at my church was going to also include journaling. I wanted to develop the discipline of journaling in a fun accountable way.

Another reason I was attracted to this "Challenge" is God's Amazing Plans Ministries foundational scripture is Jeremiah 29:11. Which is also my life verse; or as I like to call it, my inheritance verses from Jeremiah 29:11 thru verse 14, which summarized, states "God has a plan for my life, and if I seek Him I will find Him, and He will bring me back from my captivity." I wanted to find out more about these amazing plans.

What I loved about the challenge was the accountability in a verse grace giving way. I loved the daily videos of encouragement which ranged from 2-4 minutes. I appreciated how much information and encouragement was put in such a short and concise manner. Each day we were given a topical assignment to write in our journal with specific instruction, first to spend time with the Lord being still and listening to

Him. We were instructed to get into scripture, to write about our gifts and talents, to learn the father's voice, to forgive freely by writing who we needed to forgive, the offenses or defenses and the action taken to demonstrate forgiveness.

Each day I would start by listening to the video and then I would think and ponder on the assignment until I was able to sit alone and do it. I looked forward to reading the assignment and spending time with the Father every day.

On the very first day we were encouraged to find who we are in Christ Jesus. We were to read Jeremiah Chapter 1. It was a day for our Heavenly Father to reveal who we are in Him. It was life changing for me to hear and comprehend how much God loves me and my reflection of Him in me. He designed me with great purpose and I have moved one step closer to living out His amazing plans for my life through this 30-Day Challenge.

I pray each of you taking this journey discover God in a whole new way and allow Him to bless you with His love and perfect design of you.

KATRINA GALVAN
Business Executive, Hesperia, CA

Reflecting on the 30-Day Challenge: Live Out God's Amazing Plans *in Your Life, I was truly amazed to see what can unfold over the course of just one month by committing myself to intentional time with the Lord.*

I had become stuck and overwhelmed by the responsibilities of everyday life, and my closest relationships were simply out of order. From day one, I felt the presence of the Holy Spirit move me. This gave me new motivation. I was suddenly inspired again by life every morning. I could not wait to spend time in His presence!

I think we all get stuck sometimes, overwhelmed by the busyness and complications of life, that we lose sight of who we are in Christ.

This challenge became my personal revival with the Lord. Instead of coming to Him with the same old prayer requests day after day, I was spending quality time with my Savior. This shift created a space quiet and still enough to allow me to hear what the Spirit was saying. He opened my eyes so that I could see glimpses of life from His perspective. I know with certainty now that God has gifted me to be an embodiment of His peace to others. I always viewed this as weakness because it seems so passive. That, of course, is the lie of the enemy and a worldly point of view.

The armor of God is peace and I am a warrior for the one and only Prince of Peace, the daughter of the King of Kings! Wherever you are in your walk with Christ, there is no doubt in my mind and heart that if you commit to this 30-Day Challenge, if you are intentional and fully surrender yourself, this study will be life changing.

Praise God for Tamara and her willingness to move boldly in faith to lead others in a deeper relationship with the Lord!

God Bless!

BLANCA CISNEROS
Founder and Life Coach, FreeToBe Life Coaching, Corona, CA

I have known Tamara Doss for many years. We are close friends and work together in partnership helping one another grow our Ministries. She is an amazing woman of God with a big heart to help people grow in the Lord, be overcomers and live victorious lives.

I have had the honor and privilege to participate in God's Amazing Plans 30-Day Challenge. *The 30-Day Challenge has been an amazing experience. I enjoyed the daily videos along with Tamara's teachings which were insightful. Her instruction, direction and guiding questions helped facilitate the journaling time with The Lord. Practicing the listening prayer to hear what God had to say to me personally was encouraging. The daily accountability has been very helpful, and the good thing is you can jump in at any time, it is ongoing. Daily practice overtime becomes a habit. I encourage everyone to participate in this Challenge. You will be Blessed!*

One of my favorite scriptures is Isaiah 1:18, God says, "Come now let us reason together." It's an invitation to have a conversation. In this testimony below, you will see that the Lord first validated me by saying I understand. Then the Lord reminded me of the miracles he had done in my marriage (we have been married 32 years), then He gave me counsel as to what to do; then edified me. I love that God can address areas in our lives in a loving, non-traumatic way that promotes healing and growth.

Testimony Day 9 of the Challenge "Search Your Heart of All Things Not of God." Psalms 139:23-24 The Lord and I began a dialog.

I prayed and asked the Lord to Search My Heart, "Lord search me, search my heart and if there is anything you want to shine the light on or illuminate any area in my life that is not right with you, please speak to me."

The Lord said, "Your attitude toward your husband." I shared with the Lord how hard it has been for me. He said," I understand the journey with him has been challenging."

"Love him as I love him, see him through the lenses of my eyes, how I see him. Look through my eyes and see the miracles I have done. The healing of his depression. Restoration of what the locust had eaten and taken away from you both. Healing and restoration of your marriage, making all things new. Returning to joy and connection through Immanuel Prayer with Me. Restoration and new relationships being formed with his children."

"Your husband is a good and righteous man. He is my son. He has a sincere, honest and transparent heart. See him through my eyes, love him as I love him."

Then the Lord began to give me His counsel as to what to do. "Do not be afraid to surrender and let your guard down. Do not give up doing what is right. Do not hold back kindness for fear that his old man (old ways) will come back. Your faith in Me that I could do a miracle in your marriage, your obedience in following Me and trusting Me has caused the transformation in your marriage. Continue in faith doing what is right."

Thank You Lord. I am grateful for your gentle involvement in my journey of life; leading and guiding me back to love, joy and peace. I Thank You and Praise you for your miracle in my marriage!

May God bless each of you in powerful ways as you journey through this 30-Day Challenge as you search and discover your amazing plan!

LEAH WILLIAMS
Administrative Assistant, Corona CA

I had been sick and became physically tired, which caused emotional exhaustion. I had been missing work, social events, church and bible study. I was secluded. This led to feeling spiritually disconnected, like I was floating and struggling through each day. My heart desired to be in alignment with the Lord's path. I decided to accept God's Amazing Plans 30-Day Challenge because I needed to purposefully seek the Lord's direction. Anything I do to draw closer to the Lord draws me closer to His path. I saw God show up. He met me right where I was and honored my desire to hear Him. I will be honest, some days were more difficult than others, so it took me longer to complete certain topics. This is different for everyone because God's plans are unique for each person. We all have various experiences through our life journeys. The cool thing is, there are no wrong answers. It is a very personal journey and I am learning to embrace mine.

I was doing great until Day 5: Search for the Truth. I was sorting through my struggles, burdens, and negative beliefs so the Lord could reveal His Truths. I had a superficial list and was feeling blocked from hearing God's voice. I put my journal down for a few days, which turned into a week! Finally, I sought Tamara for prayer.

As we sat together, a verse came to mind Psalm 27:10 "Though my father and mother forsake me, the Lord will receive me." My parents have never forsaken me, so I did not think this verse was relevant. It *came up two more times, so I decided to try reading it in different versions. It was obvious that I needed to figure out how it applied to me. The New Living Translation had the answer: "Even if my father and mother abandon me, the Lord will hold me close." The Holy Spirit opened my heart, unveiling a wound I had forgotten about. A year prior I had been hurt by someone I trusted, leaving me feeling alone and abandoned. When I had originally reflected on it, I realized they probably had no idea they had hurt me, so I opted not to discuss it further. I thought I had moved forward, but my heart said otherwise. I had built a wall around my heart, which slowly turned me away from people, until I was disconnected.*

The verse is not just about a father and mother, but about anyone you love and trust. My love language is physical touch, so hearing the specific words "the Lord will hold me close" spoke directly to my heart. As I prayed and processed through my feelings I was reminded of the truth: humans will make mistakes and hurt me, but the Lord will never let me go. I continued with the challenge until Day 10 and at that point I felt the need to stop. Today I feel connected to God again even though I did not complete the challenge. Since participating, I have felt tremendous healing. I am seeing God's plans for me as doors open and close. These doors are in alignment with what I experienced in Day 1 and Day 6. My biggest struggles were making time, being still, and pushing through when it was out of my comfort zone. There was never shame or condemnation for getting off track, just encouragement not to give up. I have started the challenge again and look forward to more growth and direction.

I absolutely recommend God's Amazing Plans 30-Day Challenge. If you do not know the Lord, that's okay. This study is written in such a way that you will learn who He is and of His crazy love for you. If you already know Him, then it will draw you closer while nurturing personal growth and direction. No matter your circumstances, I urge you to investigate this challenge. There are so many lies and far too much hate in this world, let God speak truth and love into your life.

KARI BANGSTON
Legal Assistant, Boise ID

When asked to participate in the 30-Day Spiritual Challenge I was both excited and a bit nervous. I was excited because I was looking forward to what God would reveal to me as he always does when I am intent on listening and spending alone time with Him. I was nervous because I knew I would have a new topic each day to listen and pray over, and with my type A personality, I was worried how I would complete each day because I have the personality type that must check off the box and not leave a day unfinished. However, God used this time to work on my personality and breakthrough in an area I was holding out on even though I felt God and I had resolved this issue in my heart.

Learning to stay put is one of the hardest acts of obedience I can think of for a type A personality. I am always tempted to run with a thought, emotion, or out of a sense of obligation. It was during the 30-Day Challenge that I learned to stay put, pray, journal and listen. I learned that stepping back, removing my desires, emotions or other expectations, was far more important than being ready for the next day. For me, this really hit home on Day 22 "Trusting Whole Heartedly in God." I find myself in a season of singleness with so many desires and needs in my heart; so, trusting whole heartedly in God became a struggle. I listed in my journal my heart's desires and needs on one side of my journal and waited for God to speak. I waited and waited three days before I felt the scripture start to flow. As hard as it was to resolve not to move until I heard it was worth it. The answers came in the form of scripture verses like Jeremiah 29:10-11, Proverbs 18:16

and Habakkuk 2:3. Though the verse on waiting wasn't exactly what I was hoping for, I am learning to wait and to be expectant. But then days 23, 24, and 25 came so quick and on one day that I found myself back on schedule. The funny part was by this time I had resolved that I would wait for God and if I didn't finish the Challenge on time I would be fine with that, too.

My greatest breakthrough, though, happened early on and I believe prepared me to receive and be open to what God would speak and reveal to me throughout the rest of the month. It happened on Day 11. "Forgive Freely." You see, God had been preparing me for a year to verbally forgive my ex-husband and to ask his forgiveness for the part I too played in our divorce. Divorce is two sided, regardless who files. By the time it is over, hurt words are spoken, hearts are broken, and families are divided. God wanted me to be actionable in my forgiveness. He had spoken to me several times in the past year to go to my ex-husband and make right the division between us. But I always quenched the Spirit by telling myself that I had forgiven him in my heart and that was enough. God wants obedience.

I had been attending the Global Leadership Summit, and honestly hadn't had the time that morning to look at the day's topic. But when Bill Hybels said, "When I say the word forgiveness, and a name pops into your head, I am going to pray while you work up the nerve to make that call, that text, or email, offering up forgiveness", I knew today would be the day I would call my ex-husband. I didn't hesitate, I went straight to the car and asked if I could text it. God said, "NO." So, I called, and it went to voicemail. I asked forgiveness for the part I played in the divorce and forgave him for his part. He is remarried, and I felt God tell me to wish him the best in his new marriage and ask blessing over his new family.

Then I offered to meet and start working on the reconciliation that Jesus calls us to because I didn't like the division in our family. I wish I could tell you that he called and accepted; but, dear brother or sister reading this testimony, the freedom I have experienced is unexplainable. The enemy's accusations have been silenced because my motive for doing this was true and right and I no longer have any hurt feelings lingering over our divorce or his remarriage. The freedom was worth facing the fear and acting in obedience. When I got home to do my daily challenge and journal that night and saw that the day's topic was forgiveness, Tamara's message just reaffirmed that whole process. It was just a blessed and awesome confirmation. It is one of those treasured moments that I will treasure as I continue to walk in my faith with God.

I pray that each person who takes this 30-Day Challenge will not only hear from God but see tremendous breakthroughs in their own life. I also pray that if you are like me and feel the need to never leave a task unfinished or blank not filled in, you will take a breath, resolve to stay put, and listen. Don't move forward until you hear, get together with others and pray with them over an unresolved issue or topic. Let God speak to you and then do what He asks.

Blessings, fellow Brothers and Sisters as you journey over the next 30 days to discover your amazing plans.

Daily Preparation and Expectations for this 30-Day Challenge of Discovering God's Amazing Plan for Your Life.

1. Dedicate a set time each day to spend at least 30 minutes with the Lord for these exercises. You can designate more time if you desire but create at least 30 minutes a day in your schedule to take this Challenge.
2. Identify a special meeting place or prayer closet to spend this intimate time with your Abba Father.
3. Grab your Bible for easy reference and reading.
4. Turn on some of your favorite worship music to calm your soul.
5. Invite the Holy Spirit to dwell in your presence.
6. Journal daily to document your experiences, conversations and insights directly with and from your Father God. Journaling is evidence of His presence and love for you. Do not edit His words or conversations with you. Write it all down.
7. Check in every day at **www.GodsAmazingPlans.com**, look for the *30-Day Challenge* and each day's encouraging video from Tamara to gain her perspective on the daily assignment.
8. Create or join a bible study, accountability group or small circle of friends on this Challenge to share your experiences from the journey and to hold one another accountable each day.
9. Get involved with and follow Amazing Life Ministries online at **www.GodsAmazingPlans.com** and Social Media (*God's Amazing Plans and Amazing Life Ministries*). Check to see if we are currently offering a 30-Day Challenge accountability and encouragement group so you can participate with us.
10. Pray for God to reveal Himself to you in new ways and to bring you awareness and clarity of His amazing plans for your life.

**The best place to start is right where you are.
Answer these questions before you begin:**

1. Why have you chosen to do this 30-Day Challenge: Live Out God's Amazing Plans?

2. Do you believe God has a plan for your life? If yes, what do you believe it is? If no, why do you think that?

3. What are you hoping to get or experience through this 30-Day journey?

4. Do you currently hear the voice of God? How and When? If not, why do you think you cannot hear His voice?

5. Do you obey God when He asks you to do something?

6. How much time daily or weekly do you currently spend with the Lord? In prayer? In His word? In worship?

7. Are you holding onto pain, regret, and/or anger from your past? Explain.

ARE
YOU
READY
TO CHANGE
YOUR
LIFE?

30-DAY CHALLENGE

Live Out

God's Amazing Plans

DAY 1

FIND WHO YOU ARE IN CHRIST JESUS

DAY 1: FIND WHO YOU ARE IN CHRIST JESUS

It's DAY 1 of the Challenge. Congratulations, you are here! Today, we are going to FIND WHO YOU ARE IN CHRIST JESUS. I want you to spend 15 to 30 minutes in meditation, quiet and reading the Bible starting at Jeremiah Chapter 1.

In Jeremiah 1:5 God spoke to Jeremiah *"Before I formed you in the womb I knew you, before you were born I set you apart; I appointed you as a prophet to the nations."*

He is speaking to you too. He knew you. He created you. And He preordained you with your amazing plan before you were even created in your Mother's womb. When we begin to grasp that power and understanding of who God is and how much time, love, and detail He put into creating each one of us, we can begin to grasp that all things are possible with God, as spoken by Jesus.

In Matthew 19:26, Jesus looked at them and said, *"With man this is impossible, but with God all things are possible."* This is where we choose to start our challenge on DAY 1. We begin this journey by understanding God's plan for us before we were even born, and that all things are possible with God!

Today, we will seek Him for His perspective of His amazing plan designed specifically for our purpose here on earth, and for enlightenment of the gifts He provided us so that we may carry out that amazing plan and purpose.

CHALLENGE: Today, after reading Jeremiah 1, place your hand on the Bible as you have it opened to the book of Jeremiah. Surrender yourself to God's will. Surrender yourself to His plan for you. Give yourself permission to be childlike in faith and vulnerable to ALL possibilities of what He wants to share with you. Be prepared to spend time with your Father and expect to hear His voice and learn His immeasurable love for you.

Don't hesitate on your hearing or writing. If you hear Him tell you something, write it down without thought or judgement. We will ponder it later. Today (and every day) will be a day of no holding back, no second guessing, and no doubting it is your Father speaking to you. If it is kind and loving, if it is affirming and gentle, if it is encouraging and reassuring, it is your Father.

It is not your job to edit your Father's love, perspective and truth spoken to you. Don't edit what you hear, or you will not hear Him clearly and you will begin to close off your communication with Him. Editing His words is tuning out His voice.

Today, pray to your Heavenly Father about what He wants to reveal to you about WHO YOU ARE IN HIM. Listen intently and write down the key words, phrases or pictures as He describes them to you. Write down His truth as He shares it with you about who He created you to be and how you resemble Jesus Christ himself. Especially write down the characteristics of how He created you in His image. You are in Him and He is in you.

I will continue to provide you with guidance throughout this 30-Day journey. You will grow through this process as you learn and practice the skill of quieting your soul to hear the voice of God. Enjoy today and the next 30 days as you encounter your Father.

Be blessed and be blessing to others as you identify who you are in Christ and live out your amazing plans.

SPEND 30 MINUTES IN MEDITATION, PRAYER AND READING HIS WORD. ASK GOD TO REVEAL TO YOU WHO YOU ARE IN HIM. LIST OUT HIS KEY WORDS, PHRASES OR VISUALS.

(Watch video encouragement at www.GodsAmazingPlans.com)

DAY 1: FIND WHO YOU ARE IN CHRIST.

FATHER REVEAL TO ME WHO I AM IN CHRIST JESUS AS YOU CREATED ME TO BE:

FATHER REVEAL TO ME WHO I AM IN CHRIST JESUS AS YOU CREATED ME TO BE:

_____
_____
_____
_____
_____
_____
_____
_____
_____
_____
_____
_____
_____
_____
_____
_____
_____
_____
_____
_____
_____
_____
_____
_____
_____
_____
_____
_____
_____
_____

FATHER REVEAL TO ME WHO I AM IN CHRIST JESUS AS YOU CREATED ME TO BE:

_____
_____
_____
_____
_____
_____
_____
_____
_____
_____
_____
_____
_____
_____
_____
_____
_____
_____
_____
_____
_____
_____
_____
_____
_____
_____
_____
_____
_____
_____
_____

WHAT REVELATION HAS GOD GIVEN YOU TODAY AS YOU SEEK WHO YOU ARE IN HIM? WRITE YOUR REVELATIONS:

WHAT REVELATION HAS GOD GIVEN YOU TODAY AS YOU SEEK WHO YOU ARE IN HIM? WRITE YOUR REVELATIONS:

DAY 2

DISCOVER YOUR PROMISES FROM GOD

DAY 2: DISCOVER YOUR PROMISES FROM GOD

It's DAY 2 of the Challenge and today we are going to DISCOVER OUR PROMISES FROM GOD. The Bible is the word of God and is powerful and life changing. It's important to know that the promises of God are true, useful and directly from Him. We learn in 2 Timothy 3:16 *"All Scripture is God-breathed and is useful for teaching, rebuking, correcting and training in righteousness."* With this promise of God in hand, we can be assured that what we learn in the Bible comes from Him and that it is for our good.

In the song called *Standing on the Promises of God*, by Alan Jackson, I love his words about God's promises are solid ground for our feet to rest. You can stand firmly upon His promises for eternity without worry, doubt, fear or hesitation. We will shout and sing God's praises as we stand on the promises of God as written by Mr. Jackson.

Today, we are going to search for our promises from God that we can stand on for a moment, a day, a season and for a lifetime.

CHALLENGE: Spend 10 minutes in silent prayer before your Father. Ask God what promises He wants to reveal to you. Pray for His divine guidance. Then search the Bible to discover His promises through specific verses that speak to your current situation or circumstances. Search for at least three promises that address your struggles. You can search by topic in the back of your Bible to ensure truth be spoken directly to you on your issues. You will use your promises to destroy the enemy and praise God as you stand firmly on His words and truth.

Write each of your promises in this journal, on pages 45 and 46 under DAY 2 DISCOVER YOUR PROMISES FROM GOD.

Next, ask the Holy Spirit to reveal to you the depth of these promises so you can firmly plant your feet on them under all trials, tribulation and troubles that come your way. Journal every conversation, insight and wisdom the Spirit is revealing to you. Don't leave anything in your head—put it all on paper as evidence. This is evidence that you have been in the presence of God. He is speaking directly to you through His Holy Spirit and He desires to have a deep personal relationship with you just like He had with His son Jesus.

Today, on DAY 2, we choose to stand on the promises of God. I encourage you to choose every day to stand on God's solid promises, especially these that He shares with you today as you seek Him. These are His promises spoken directly to you for such a time as this.

Be blessed and be a blessing to others as they watch you stand on the promises of God through difficult and challenging circumstances. You will witness to them from solid ground.

SPEND 30 MINUTES IN MEDITATION, PRAYER AND READING HIS WORD. ON THE LEFT SIDE, WRITE THE CIRCUMSTANCES YOU ARE FACING OR HAVE FACED IN THE PAST. ASK GOD TO REVEAL TO YOU THREE BIBLE VERSES THAT ARE HIS PROMISES TO YOU REGARDING THESE CIRCUMSTANCES. WRITE THEM DOWN ON THE RIGHT SIDE OF THE PAGE.

(Watch video encouragement at www.GodsAmazingPlans.com)

DAY 2: DISCOVER YOUR PROMISES FROM GOD

CIRCUMSTANCES: **3 PROMISES TO STAND ON:**

CIRCUMSTANCES: **3 PROMISES TO STAND ON:**

CIRCUMSTANCES:

3 PROMISES TO STAND ON:

DAY 3

CLAIM YOUR VICTORIES & BLESSINGS

DAY 3: CLAIM YOUR VICTORIES AND BLESSINGS

I pray you have found time to commit to the Lord and have delighted in the Lord's presence each day. It takes 21 days to change your brain and 66 days to create a new habit, so I pray this will become a lifestyle for you. If for some reason you haven't gotten started or you are having a difficult time, start today. You won't regret it. You will be blessed, and His Holy Spirit will transform your life.

DAY 3 is CLAIMING YOUR VICTORIES AND BLESSINGS! Victories and blessings can be associated with protection and happiness. God's blessings protect us and guide us to the path of happiness and righteousness. Here are a few Bible verses to remind you of the ultimate blessings promised to us. Use them as a reminder and direction to the amazing plan He created for you.

James 1:17 *"every good and perfect gift is from above, coming down from the Father of the heavenly lights, who does not change like shifting shadows."*

Deuteronomy 7:13" He *will love you, bless you, and multiply you. He will also bless the fruit of your womb and the fruit of your ground, your grain and your wine and your oil, the increase of your herds and the young of your flock, in the land that he swore to your fathers to give you."*

Psalms 1:1-3 *"Blessed is the one who does not walk in step with the wicked or stand in the way that sinners take or sit in the company of mockers, but whose delight is in the law of the LORD, and who meditates on His law day and night. That person is like a tree planted by streams of water, which yields its fruit in season and whose leaf does not wither—whatever they do prospers."*

CHALLENGE: Today, spend 15 minutes in prayer and ask God to

reveal to you the blessings He has bestowed upon you. As He shares these blessings with you, write them down in this journal on pages 52 through 55 under DAY 3 CLAIM YOUR VICTORIES. Claim the victories, blessings, good, and perfect gifts that God is desiring for your life. Don't forget our greatest gift and victory ever is the gift of SALVATIION. Praise you Jesus! We are forever grateful for your love and sacrifice. Victory is yours. Receive your blessings.

Then spend 15 more minutes reflecting on all the victories and obstacles you have overcome throughout your life. Meditate on all the mountains you have moved, all the powerful things you have seen and done through the Lord's strength. Spend time in reflection with the Lord through all your victories. Praise Him for these victories He has declared over you.

God's plan for your life is one of goodness, fullness, greatness, kindness, joyfulness and thankfulness. The key to unlocking the door to blessings begins with a heart of gratitude. Celebrate what God has blessed you with and what He has helped you overcome. Don't hesitate while journaling. Go back through every year of your life and don't miss a detail of His greatness and victories in your life. You are blessed and today we claim our victories!

On DAY 3 we choose to spend time reminiscing with our Abba Father and enjoy His presence as we learn to recognize and claim our victories and blessings through His love for us and His mighty power in our lives.

Be blessed and be a blessing to others as they see you claim your victories through Christ Jesus. Live in God's fullness every day.

SPEND 30 MINUTES IN MEDITATION, PRAYER AND READING HIS WORD. ASK GOD TO REVEAL TO YOU ALL OF THE VICTORIES AND BLESSINGS YOU HAVE CONQUERED AND RECEIVED. WRITE THEM ALL DOWN.

DAY 3 CLAIM YOUR VICTORIES

VICTORIES: (obstacles overcome) **BLESSINGS:** (gifts received)

VICTORIES: (obstacles overcome) **BLESSINGS:** (gifts received)

VICTORIES: (obstacles overcome) **BLESSINGS:** (gifts received)

VICTORIES: (obstacles overcome) **BLESSINGS:** (gifts received)

DAY 4

RECOGNIZE YOUR CALLING

DAY 4: RECOGNIZE YOUR CALLING

Today is DAY 4 and we are going to RECOGNIZE OUR GOD GIVEN CALLING. What is a calling? It is God's perfect plan with a purpose that every single person has for their life. It is what God created and designed you to do. It's not just the gifts and talents he has given you, but with the desire and position to glorify God. We all have great gifts and talents, but if we don't use them to glorify God, then they are not used for His purposes. Our calling is what we are "called out" by God Almighty to do to bring honor and glory to Him and to serve others through His love.

In Ephesians 2:10 it says, *"We are God's handiwork, created in Christ Jesus to do good works, which God prepared in advance for us to do."* Woohoo! He already prepared us in advance to do good works and live out our calling, but we have a very important job. Our job is to learn to recognize our gifts, embrace our talents, and live them out for God's glory. I teach more about this in my book and bible study *"The Seven Steps to Living Out Your Amazing Plan"* in Chapter 1: Perfect Plan with Purpose, and Chapter 2: Recognize Your Gifts and Talents.

God's gift to us is our talents and our gift back to Him is using our talents to glorify Him. Today, we will learn to recognize them and find out how to use them as God instructs us. Pray over these questions and seek the Lord's guidance and perspective:

1. Can you believe that God designed you with a powerful and mighty plan? Explain.

_____

_____

_____

_____

_____

_____

2. Describe the gifts and talents that God has placed in you.

_____

_____

_____

_____

_____

_____

3. Identify circumstances that you have faced that have broken your confidence in your giftings?

_____

_____

_____

_____

_____

_____ Ask God to restore you.

4. What amazing plans for your life have you allowed the enemy to destroy?

_____

_____

_____

_____

_____

_____ Ask God to restore you.

5. What do you desire to accomplish in your life for God?

_____

_____

_____

_____

_____

_____

CHALLENGE: Today, on one side of your journal, write a list of all your qualities, talents, gifts, and passions. On the other side, write how you can use those gifts to glorify God. Then match those gifts and talents to your dreams of how you want to change the world, your family, community and your circles of influence. Spend time in prayer asking God to reveal to you your calling and purpose that He designed specifically for you.

Embrace God's truth and promises. Step into your gifts, talents and passions to fulfill His plans for your life. Believe that you are a unique, special, gifted child of God, with a great purpose and plan appointed and pre-ordained by your Abba Father. He is the master designer of life and you are His masterpiece.

In John 15:16 it says, *"You did not choose me, but I chose you and appointed you so that you might go and bear fruit; fruit that will last, so that whatever you ask in my name, the Father will give you."* Pray over this verse and listen to what your Father is sharing with you. Write it all down in your journal under DAY 4 RECOGNIZE YOUR CALLING.

Be blessed and be a blessing to others as they watch you recognize and live out your God given calling.

SPEND 30 MINUTES IN MEDITATION, PRAYER AND READING HIS WORD. ASK GOD TO REVEAL TO YOU YOUR QUALITIES, TALENTS, GIFTINGS AND PASSIONS (Q.T.G.P.). WRITE THEM DOWN. THEN, PRAY AND WRITE ON THE RIGHT SIDE OF YOUR JOURNAL HOW YOU CAN USE THEM FOR GOD.

(Watch the encouraging video at www.GodsAmazingPlans.com)

DAY 4: RECOGNIZE YOUR CALLING

Q.T.G.P.:   **HOW TO USE THEM FOR GOD:**

_____ | _____
_____ | _____
_____ | _____
_____ | _____

Q.T.G.P.:   **HOW TO USE THEM FOR GOD:**

Q.T.G.P.:   **HOW TO USE THEM FOR GOD:**

Q.T.G.P.:   **HOW TO USE THEM FOR GOD:**

DAY 5

SEARCH FOR THE TRUTH

DAY 5: SEARCH FOR THE TRUTH

On the DAY 1 encouraging video you watched on www.GodsAmazingPlans.com, I told you that no one has the authority to tell you who you are, except God! Well, today we are going to SEARCH FOR HIS TRUTH, because not only is He the only one who can tell you who you are, but He is truly the only one who can tell you what to do if you desire to live in His will.

God is the only one who can comfort you deep enough to truly heal you from the inside out. God is the only one where you can find the peace that surpasses all understanding. God is the only one who can guide you to lay beside still waters in troubled times. God is the only one who loves you unconditionally, forgives you of all your sins, and pours grace and mercy over your life every day you live. He is the only one who can restore you to your birthright of greatness. He is the only one who has sacrificed His son Jesus to redeem you and given you the greatest gift ever, Salvation.

On DAY 5 we are going to SEARCH FOR THE TRUTH; God's truth and nothing but God's truth! In Psalm 25:5 it says, *"Lead me in your truth and teach me, for you are the God of my salvation; for you I wait all day long."* Today, let us seek His truth and allow God to teach us and to lead us to everlasting truth.

The only way we can search for truth is by reading His word and asking the Holy Spirit to help us to hear from God what He wants us to know from His words. Then we will be able to hear the truth of our Father's heart, and instructions from His mind, His eyes, His plan and His great love for us. There is no other way to know God's truth than to read the word of God and through the presence of His Holy Spirit. If you do not practice this every day, you will be living in a world of lies and not grounded in truth. When we do not have our "Belt of Truth" on, as we learn about in Ephesians 6, we begin to believe lies as truth and we become confused, exhausted, overwhelmed, and defeated by lies. Seek

God's truth today and be restored and strengthened.

Today's challenge is to identify an issue or struggle in your life. It could be physical, emotional, mental, financial or spiritual. It should not be a challenge from Day 2 when we sought His promises; this is a bigger struggle you have been facing. One that has lived deep inside of you for years. It may be chains and bondage from your past and a lie of the enemy that was taken root in your heart and has prevented you from living out your amazing plan because you believed you were not worthy.

CHALLENGE: On the left side of your journal on pages 69 through 71, write your burdens, struggles and negative beliefs about yourself. You must first spend time in prayer and surrender to really dig deep to see and know what God reveals to you about your heart and life. Remember, we keep no secrets from God, He knows everything about us. Real transformation in us begins when we confess our sins, struggles and hurts so that we can ask for God's divine and supernatural healing and restoration.

As we begin to seek God's truth, we destroy the enemy's lies. John 8:32 says "...and you will know the truth, and the truth will set you free." This truth is God's love for us. Truth is God's powerful love that can and will set us free when we seek Him and embrace His truth and love for us.

Somewhere throughout your life you have been hurt and perhaps have forgotten God's immeasurable love for you. Your birthright has been stolen and distorted from the truth of being a perfect child of God, created in His image, worthy of all that He has created for you. You are sons and daughters of the King. You are royalty. Today is the day to break down those lies that have scared you and start your new life. We are going to search for guidance from the one and only source who knows us and how perfectly He designed us. He is the one and only source who knows how to speak truth into our lives about who we really are and who we are created to be.

First, take several minutes to pray for God to reveal His truth behind those burdens and lies you wrote down about yourself. Pray for clarity and understanding of His truth in your life. Search out the Bible for the truth about your burdens, emotional scars or challenges. I want you to search for NEW scriptures that you have not yet claimed before as your own. Keep searching for new ones. Read as many scriptures as your time allows. Then pray over the verses that God wants to teach you truth on. Be open to listening to His direction. You might even discover it is not what you have believed in the past. Write it all down.

Remember, DO NOT edit God's perspective, voice and love for you. When we start editing God's voice and second guessing and questioning His truth and His love for us, we start slowly turning it off because we are not trusting Him. We are not trusting that He has a good plan for our lives and we are not trusting that He is a good Father. He is a good Father who loves you and is desiring a relationship with you. Learn to listen intently for His truth and receive His love though the words He is speaking directly to you.

In John 18:37 *"Then Pilate said to him, 'So you are a king?' Jesus answered, 'You say that I am a king. For this purpose, I was born, and for this purpose, I have come into the world—to bear witness to the truth. Everyone who is of the truth listens to my voice."*

CHALLENGE: Today, on DAY 5, we choose to SEARCH OUT OUR FATHER'S TRUTH. We choose to believe in His love for us. We choose to believe that He is a good Father and to believe that He can do all things! We choose to search for the truth and recognize His truth about us. We will not settle for the lies of the enemy from this day forward but always seek His truth about us.

Be blessed and be a blessing to others as they watch you search for the truth in your life's difficult circumstances and you remain unshakable through His love for you. Stand firm in His truth!

SPEND 30 MINUTES IN MEDITATION, PRAYER AND READING HIS WORD. ASK GOD TO REVEAL TO YOU THE BURDENS YOU HAVE BEEN CARRYING THAT YOU NEED TO LAY DOWN. WRITE THEM DOWN. THEN WRITE HIS TRUTHS THAT DESTROY THE LIES AND GIVE YOU FREEDOM AND REST. WRITE THEM ALL DOWN.

(Watch the encouraging video at www.GodsAmazingPlans.com)

DAY 5: SEARCH FOR THE TRUTH.

BURDENS TO LAY DOWN: **TRUTHS TO PICK UP:**

BURDENS TO LAY DOWN: **TRUTHS TO PICK UP:**

BURDENS TO LAY DOWN: **TRUTHS TO PICK UP:**

DAY 6

LEARN YOUR FATHER'S VOICE

DAY 6: LEARN YOUR FATHER'S VOICE

It's DAY 6 and you are a blessed child of God! I am so excited for those who are faithfully walking day by day and being blessed by the Spirit of God through this Challenge. Today, on DAY 6, we are going to LEARN OUR FATHER'S VOICE. We are going to press in and become the sheep that know our Father's voice and would recognize it anywhere, anytime, and in all circumstances.

It says in John 10:27, *"My sheep listen to my voice; I know them, and they follow me."* See how God says we must LISTEN to His voice to follow Him. You can't follow Him any other way, but to learn, recognize, and tune into the voice of God. So today, we are taking on that challenge: to increase our power of listening to our loving Father. We will speak less as we will begin to listen more.

The only way to learn how to recognize and know your Father's voice is by spending time in His presence, conversing with Him, and most importantly, listening to His love for you. You will know His voice and truth by His love, grace, mercy, and goodness for your life. Today, during prayer time, I encourage you to speak less, way less, and listen more intently for His assurances. Today will be a day of prayer and meditation to learn to listen attentively in complete silence to His voice.

The *first key* to hearing God's voice is to go to a QUIET PLACE and STILL YOUR OWN THOUGHTS AND EMOTIONS. Psalm 46:10 encourages us to *"be still, let go, cease striving, and know that He is God."*

In Psalm 37:7 we are called to *"Be still before the Lord and wait patiently for Him."* There is a deep inner knowing in our spirit that each of us can experience when we quiet our flesh and our minds. Practicing the art of biblical meditation helps us silence the outer noise and distractions clamoring for our attention. We must clear the clutter and be still before the Lord to hear His voice clearly.

74

The _second key_ to hearing God's voice is to FIX THE EYES OF YOUR HEART UPON JESUS as you pray; seeing, hearing and knowing the Spirit, dreams and visions of Almighty God.

Habakkuk was looking for vision as he prayed. He opened the eyes of his heart and investigated the spirit world to see what God wanted to show him. We will begin to seek Jesus's heart of how He loves us and seek His eyes to see the things He sees, and to seek His ears to hear the things He hears. Then, we will begin to clearly hear the voice of God and know His thoughts and heart.

The _third key_ to hearing God's voice is recognizing that God's voice in your heart often sounds like a flow of SPONTANEOUS THOUGHTS. Therefore, when I want to hear from God, I tune my heart to have an encounter and listen for spontaneous thoughts of His. Sometimes He may just give me a word, a phrase, or sometimes a complete sentence or direction, but most of the time He gives me His spontaneous thoughts.

I often hear from God in one-word commands signaling me that He wants to talk with me or make me aware of something He is working on in my life. He speaks one-word commands like "Go," "Now," "Change," "Stop," or even a person's name or a problem. But over time I have come to learn from Him that these words are just signals to get my attention. He is drawing my attention to press into Him and to direct me to seek what He wants me to do, where He wants me to go and when He wants me to do it.

God has always spoken through dreams and visions, and He specifically said that they would come to those upon whom the Holy Spirit is poured out (Acts 2:1-4, 17).

The _fourth key_ to hearing God's voice is in TWO-WAY JOURNALING, the writing out of your prayers to Him and God's responses to you. Journaling your conversations with God brings

75

great freedom and power in hearing God's voice and being fiercely obedient. Journaling God's words is evidence of His presence.

God told Habakkuk to record the vision (Hab. 2:2). This was not an isolated command. The Scriptures record many examples of individual people's prayers, and God's replies such as in Psalms, to many of the prophets, and in Revelation. I have found that obeying this final principle of recording the visions and conversations with the Lord amplified my confidence in my ability to hear God's voice so that I could finally make living out His initiatives a way of life. I know His voice and so I follow Him.

CHALLENGE: Today, on DAY 6, we LEARN OUR FATHER'S VOICE. We choose to go before the Lord, pray and journal our prayers to Him and then listen for His response to us. Go to a quiet place, still yourself and your mind, journal a prayer that weighs heavily on your heart. Fix your eyes on the heart of Jesus, wait for God to speak. Then write down all the spontaneous thoughts He shares. Enjoy this special day that the Lord has made and know that He is waiting for you. He desires to speak with you.

Be blessed and be a blessing to others as you learn your Father's voice and share it freely with those around you. His voice is powerful, and He created you to hear Him and know His voice above all other voices. Bless others with the power of His voice.

SPEND 30 MINUTES IN MEDITATION, PRAYER AND READING HIS WORD. WRITE A PRAYER OF THANKSGIVING TO YOUR FATHER AND ASK GOD TO REVEAL TO YOU HIS VOICE, HIS LOVE FOR YOU AND WHAT HE WANTS YOU TO KNOW IN HIS RESPONSE TO YOUR PRAYER.

(Watch the encouraging video at www.GodsAmazingPlans.com)

DAY 6: LEARN YOUR FATHER'S VOICE

DAY 6: LEARN YOUR FATHER'S VOICE
YOUR PRAYER TO GOD:

YOUR PRAYER TO GOD:

_____

_____

_____

_____

_____

_____

_____

_____

_____

_____

_____

_____

_____

_____

_____

_____

_____

_____

_____

_____

_____

_____

_____

_____

_____

_____

_____

_____

_____

GOD'S RESPONSE TO YOU: (Be still and listen intently)

GOD'S RESPONSE TO YOU: (Be still and listen intently)

_____
_____
_____
_____
_____
_____
_____
_____
_____
_____
_____
_____
_____
_____
_____
_____
_____
_____
_____
_____
_____
_____
_____
_____
_____
_____
_____
_____

GOD'S RESPONSE TO YOU: (Be still and listen intently)

DAY 7

KNOW
GOOD
FROM
EVIL

DAY 7: KNOW GOOD FROM EVIL

CONGRATULATIONS! Week 1 of The Challenge is complete, just three more weeks to go: 7 days down, 21 days to go. Don't quit. It takes 21 days to retrain your brain and 66 days to create a new habit and a new way of living, so push through and make it happen. Spending time with Jesus every day will change your life.

Today, on DAY 7, we are going to focus on KNOWING GOOD FROM EVIL. It is important to always recognize good from evil in all situations and conversations you encounter. God is good, and the devil is evil. Sometimes the enemy likes to confuse us by looking and feeling like good, disguising himself as good, but He is not good. He has no intention for you to grow, flourish, or produce fruit. He wants to kill your roots, he wants to steal your fruit, he wants to destroy your destiny and your amazing plan.

Today, don't be fooled by what looks good or feels good, when really it is evil from the devil and meant to harm you. I encourage you to pray to God and ask Him what He would like to reveal to you about a lie in your life that you have been believing. Ask Him to reveal to you a specific lie, then ask Him to help you destroy that lie and seek the truth of His goodness for you.

Jeremiah 12:2 says *"You have planted them, they have also taken root; they grow, they have even produced fruit. You are near to their lips but far from their mind."*

Today, we are going to pray for our Father God to empower us to keep Him near to our minds, not just our lips. We cannot just talk about God's love, grace, mercy, power and victory without having truth and goodness planted firmly in our minds and hearts.

To destroy evil, we can read Matthew 15:13 and learn. It says, *"But He answered and said, every plant which my heavenly Father did not plant shall be uprooted."* Let's go together and seek the enemy's planting in our life and uproot it permanently.

In Matthew 3:10, *"The axe is already laid at the root of the trees; therefore, every tree that does not bear good fruit is cut down and thrown into the fire."* Yes, let our trees that are not bearing good fruit be destroyed today so we can begin to allow God to grow us strong, stable, fertile and bear much good fruit to glorify Him.

Hope of producing good fruit in our lives through God is found in Job 14:7-9, *"For there is hope for a tree, when it is cut down, that it will sprout again, and its shoots will not fail. Though its roots grow old in the ground and its stump dies in the dry soil, at the scent of water it will flourish and put forth sprigs like a plant."*

And in Jeremiah 17:7-8, the Bible tells us, *"Blessed is the man who trusts in the Lord and whose trust is the Lord. For he will be like a tree planted by the water, that extends its roots by a stream and will not fear when the heat comes; but its leaves will be green, and it will not be anxious in a year of drought, nor cease to yield fruit."* Hallelujah! Rest assured that God will restore us and help us to know good from evil. And through His Spirit we will yield fruit.

In Isaiah 61:3 We are promised restoration and rebirth. *"He will provide and bestow on us a crown of beauty instead of ashes, the oil of joy instead of mourning, and a garment of praise instead of a spirit of despair. They will be called oaks of righteousness, a planting of the Lord for the display of His splendor."*

Today on DAY 7 of the Challenge, we choose to trust in the Lord, to become people whose trust is the Lord. We are going to recognize, become keenly aware of, and KNOW GOOD FROM EVIL in our life that is trying to take root in us. We will no longer allow evil into our lives because we choose to trust in our God, to be planted by His living water and bear much fruit. We have Him on our lips, and even more importantly, in our minds and in our hearts!

CHALLENGE: Under DAY 7 in your journal below, on the left side of your paper write the lie, or many lies, distractions and burdens you have allowed to take root in your heart over the years. Pray for God to reveal them all so you can surrender them to Him today, to uproot and remove them all. Then spend time in prayer asking God to reveal the truth. List the truth on the right side of the paper. Then ask Him to uproot those lies and destroy them on your paper! Uproot them and replace them with His truth and goodness!

Be blessed today and be a blessing to others as you learn to know good from evil and celebrate the good and destroy the evil.

SPEND 30 MINUTES IN MEDITATION, PRAYER AND READING HIS WORD. ASK GOD TO REVEAL TO YOU THE LIES OF THE ENEMY YOU HAVE BEEN BELIEVING. WRITE THEM DOWN IN YOUR JOURNAL AND THEN WRITE ALL OF GOD'S TRUTH SO YOU CAN BEGIN TO LEARN GOOD FROM EVIL. KNOW TRUTH AND HIS TRUTH WILL SET YOU FREE.

(Watch the encouraging video at www.GodsAmazingPlans.com)

DAY 7: KNOW GOOD FROM EVIL

DEVIL'S EVIL LIES: **GOD'S GOOD TRUTH:**

DEVIL'S EVIL LIES: **GOD'S GOOD TRUTH:**

DEVIL'S EVIL LIES: **GOD'S GOOD TRUTH:**

DEVIL'S EVIL LIES: **GOD'S GOOD TRUTH:**

DAY 8

BE ON GUARD AGAINST THE ENEMY

DAY 8: BE ON GUARD AGAINST THE ENEMY

Today, on DAY 8, we are going to BE ON GUARD AGAINST THE ENEMY. Learn to keep your eyes and ears open to where the enemy is trying to mislead you. Be on guard. Do not allow him to kill, steal, or destroy the mighty plans God has prepared for you.

You must always be on guard and prepared to fight the enemy at every moment. Never assume you are prepared if you have not begun with a prayer of protection and suited up for battle. When you begin to recognize the enemy's assaults, immediately act and claim your birthright of freedom and victory over yourself.

You were created with a perfect plan, and today, I want you to declare and reclaim your God-given birthright of a joyful, peaceful, loving, successful, happy and powerful life to help impact others around you and to glorify your God for all to see.

In Ephesians 6:10-18 we read about the Armor of God and what we must do daily to gird up against the enemy. It says *"Finally, be strong in the Lord and in His mighty power. Put on the full armor of God, so that you can take your stand against the devil's schemes. For our struggle is not against flesh and blood, but against the rulers, against the authorities, against the powers of this dark world and against the spiritual forces of evil in the heavenly realms. Therefore, put on the full armor of God, so that when the day of evil comes, you may be able to stand your ground, and after you have done everything, to stand. Stand firm then, with the belt of truth buckled around your waist, with the breastplate of righteousness in place, and with your feet fitted with the readiness that comes from the gospel of peace. In addition to all this, take up the shield of faith, with which you can extinguish all the flaming arrows of the evil one. Take the helmet of salvation and the sword of the Spirit, which is the word of God. And pray in the Spirit, on all occasions with all kinds of prayers and requests. Be alert and always keep on praying for all the Lord's people."*

It is important that we realize we must do this daily in preparation for the spiritual battle in this world. We are told that the fight is not against flesh and blood, but against the rulers of the air. We must remember that girding up is not just for some days, but for every day. Every hour of every day we must be prepared and ready.

Also, we must recognize immediately upon stumbling or attack in the battle that we have failed to gird up with His suit of armor. Stop immediately and clothe up so nothing can penetrate your heart, mind, or soul. Protect yourself so that only God's love and goodness can penetrate your life, not the attacks of the enemy.

With His protection on, the enemy has no power; you are equipped to fight the battle. Remember this: The fight is fixed, but you must get back up, stand up, be ready to fight with your Spirit-filled warrior weapons. Remain on guard and be prepared.

Paul tells us to take a stand against the devil's schemes. You must get back up, stand firm, get dressed, and create an offensive posture. When we are prepared, we have the upper hand and become less shaken by the trials of this world.

CHALLENGE: Today, on DAY 8, we choose to become men and women who are wise, prepared and GUARDED UP AGAINST THE ENEMY. We choose to stand up and defend our birthright and claim our victory in the battle that has already been won. Today, write in your journal how you are getting yourself equipped for battle. You know your weaknesses, so guard up! Journal a letter to your Father about how you are going to use His power and stand firm against the enemy's schemes with each spiritual weapon.

Be blessed and be a blessing to others as you are prepared and suited for battle defending your territory and standing in the gap for those that are unaware and unprotected with God's power.

SPEND 30 MINUTES IN MEDITATION, PRAYER AND READING HIS WORD. ASK GOD TO REVEAL TO YOU THE WISDOM AND POWER BEHIND EACH PIECE OF GOD'S ARMOR. WRITE A PRAYER TO GOD TO PREPARE YOU EACH DAY FOR BATTLE. THEN WRITE OUT THE WISDOM GOD GIVES YOU FOR EACH SPIRITUAL WEAPON OF PROTECTION.

(Watch the encouraging video at www.GodsAmazingPlans.com)

DAY 8: BE ON GUARD AGAINST THE ENEMY.

PRAYER OF PREPARATION FOR BATTLE:

_____
_____
_____
_____
_____
_____
_____
_____
_____
_____
_____
_____
_____
_____
_____
_____
_____
_____
_____
_____
_____
_____
_____
_____

BELT OF *TRUTH*:

_____
_____
_____
_____
_____
_____
_____
_____
_____
_____
_____
_____

BREASTPLATE OF *RIGHTEOUSNESS*:

_____
_____
_____
_____
_____
_____
_____
_____
_____
_____
_____
_____
_____
_____

HELMET OF *SALVATION*:

_____
_____
_____
_____
_____
_____
_____
_____
_____
_____
_____
_____
_____
_____

SHOES OF *PEACE*:

_____
_____
_____
_____
_____
_____
_____
_____
_____
_____
_____
_____
_____
_____

SHEILD OF *FAITH*:

_____
_____
_____
_____
_____
_____
_____
_____
_____
_____
_____
_____
_____
_____
_____

SWORD OF THE *SPIRIT*:

_____
_____
_____
_____
_____
_____
_____
_____
_____
_____
_____

DAY 9

SEARCH YOUR HEART FOR ALL THINGS NOT OF GOD

DAY 9: SEARCH YOUR HEART FOR ALL THINGS NOT OF GOD

Today is DAY 9 and we are going to SEARCH OUR HEARTS FOR ALL THINGS NOT OF GOD. We are going to cleanse our souls of evil and replenish them with God's will. We must examine our own hearts. Better yet, we must ask God to search our hearts and empower us to remove all things not representing our new life in Christ.

Psalm 139:23-24, "*Search me, God, and know my heart; test me and know my anxious thoughts. See if there is any offensive in me and lead me in the way everlasting.*"

I encourage you to listen to "*It Is Well with My Soul*" by Kristine Demarco of Bethel and as you do, ask God to search your heart and make all things well with your soul. He can remove anger and pain from your heart, remove fear, doubt, anxiety and worry from your mind and make all things well with your soul.

Surrender your heart to the one who purifies all the old into new. Ask Him to reveal to you the things not of God and to remove them, burn them, destroy them and allow the desires of your heart to be only for God's purposes and plans.

Romans 8:27 says, "*And he who is the searcher of hearts has knowledge of the mind of the Spirit, because he is making prayers for the saints in agreement with the mind of God.*"

CHALLENGE: Today, spend 20 minutes in prayer and ask your Father to search your heart. Invite Him in to illuminate in you all the things that need to be burned away by the Holy Spirit.

Write in your journal all the things He exposes to you. Write a plan for removal next to each of them. Include what you want to exchange them for, why it is not of God's will, and what your life would look like once they are removed from your heart.

Today, DAY 9 of the Challenge is to SEARCH OUR HEARTS FOR ALL THINGS NOT OF GOD. We choose to ask God to search our hearts, to allow him deep inside of our mind, heart and soul, to reveal to us the things that He wants us to surrender to Him. We are going to lay everything at the foot of the cross so that we can be ready to receive His glory and allow Him to move us forward in our destiny. We will be ready to move from glory to glory.

Be blessed and be a blessing to others as your heart becomes restored and your soul becomes well when we remove all things not of God in our lives. Live out your plan with a cleansed heart.

PRAY, MEDITATE AND GET IN TUNE WITH YOUR FATHER'S HEART. JOURNAL THE REVELATIONS OF WHAT GOD HAS SHOWN YOU THAT IS NOT OF HIM. LET THE FIRE OF THE HOLY GHOST BURN EVIL, LIES AND DISTRACTIONS AWAY, REMOVING THEM FROM YOUR HEART, MIND AND LIFE ANYTHING THAT'S NOT OF HIM. THEN WRITE A PLAN TO REMOVE THEM FROM YOUR LIFE AND EXPERIENCE FREEDOM.

(Watch the encouraging video at www.GodsAmazingPlans.com)

DAY 9: SEARCH YOUR HEART FOR ALL THINGS NOT OF GOD.

LORD REVEAL TO ME ALL THINGS NOT OF YOU AND A PLAN TO REMOVE THEM:

_____
_____
_____
_____
_____
_____
_____
_____

LORD REVEAL TO ME ALL THINGS NOT OF YOU AND A PLAN TO REMOVE THEM:

LORD REVEAL TO ME ALL THINGS NOT OF YOU AND A PLAN TO REMOVE THEM:

_____
_____
_____
_____
_____
_____
_____
_____
_____
_____
_____
_____
_____
_____
_____
_____
_____
_____
_____
_____
_____
_____
_____
_____
_____
_____
_____
_____

DAY 10

STAND FIRM AGAINST THE WORLD

DAY 10: STAND FIRM AGAINST THE WORLD

Wow... so many breakthroughs yesterday in one of our accountability groups doing this Challenge. I was with a friend watching her experience DAY 9's Challenge and I just want to say, "Wow, God! You are such a powerful, loving, sensitive Father and you direct us in such a way that overwhelms us with great joy, laughter, tears and conviction. You encourage us to change ourselves to become the person you envisioned when you created us. Thank you, Papa!"

Today is DAY10: STAND FIRM AGAINST THE WORLD. Today you will learn to plant your feet on solid ground of the Holy One who desires for you to live victorious! Stand firm against all worldly thoughts, entrapments, misgivings and expectations. Remember that it is the "shoes of peace" we learned about in Ephesians 6 that firmly balance your feet upon the rock of salvation. When you feel the weight of the world, or that you are getting tossed by the roaring crisis of life, pray to God for guidance, to help you stand firm and keep your eyes on Him, and to ensure your shoes are strapped tightly to experience His peace.

1 Peter 5:9 tells us to *"Resist him, standing firm in the faith, because you know that the family of believers throughout the world is undergoing the same kind of sufferings."*

And in 1 Corinthians 16:13, Paul encourages us to *"Be on your guard; stand firm in the faith; be courageous; be strong."*

CHALLENGE: Today, I want you to go into prayer, meditation and worship with your Heavenly Father and ask Him to reveal to you all the things of this world that are holding you back from moving on, from advancing forward and from stepping out in faith.

Identify the things that have trapped you from your destiny and amazing plan. Identify things of this world you are watching, hearing, doing, saying and experiencing that are obstacles on your path, preventing you from living out God's will for your life. On the left side of your paper, write down every one of them. Then, place your hand on your list and pray over them. Releasing or confessing them is the first step to completely remove them from your life. Ask Papa to release them from your life, your thoughts and your actions. Ask Papa to remain in you as you stand firm.

As you ask the Lord to remove these lies, desires and obstacles from your heart, ask Him to replace them with Heavenly things only: things of goodness, things of His heart, His will for your life. Ask God to show you the future from His eyes and Heavenly perspective, you can even imagine what you would like to do instead. Then ask God if these are His desires for your life or if they are from Him. He will lead you to the truth and declare it over you.

Now, on the right side of your journal on pages 108 to 111, list out all the things He revealed to you that you could be doing instead to glorify Him. Then hold out your hand and get ready to receive His abundance of goodness.

Philippians 1:27 tells us, "*Only conduct yourselves in a manner worthy of the gospel of Christ, so that whether I come and see you or remain absent, I will hear of you that you are standing firm in one spirit, with one mind, striving together for the faith of the gospel.*"

Today, on DAY 10 of the Challenge, we choose to STAND FIRM AGAINST THIS WORLD by reflecting on our own lives through what we watch, listen to, participate in and we choose to commit to turn off, tune out, close down, and walk away from the evil traps of this world.

We will stand firm against the world and renew our mind, as instructed in Romans 12:2, "*Do not conform to the pattern of this world but be transformed by the renewing of your mind. Then you will be able to test and approve what God's will is—His good, pleasing and perfect will."* Amen!

Be blessed today in the presence of God and be a blessing to others as you stand firm against the world. People are watching you and as you choose to stand firm you will testify of God's love, strength, faithfulness and power in your life.

SPEND 30 MINUTES IN MEDITATION, PRAYER AND READING HIS WORD. ASK GOD TO HELP YOU STAND FIRM AGAINST THIS WORLD. ASK HIM TO REVEAL TO YOU ALL THE THINGS YOU NEED TO REMOVE FROM, AND ADD TO, YOUR LIFE TO STAND FIRM IN HIS WILL. WRITE THEM DOWN.

Watch the encouraging video at www.GodsAmazingPlans.com)

DAY 10: STAND FIRM AGAINST THE WORLD

WORLDLY (to remove)   **GODLY** (to add)

WORLDLY (to remove)   **GODLY** (to add)

WORLDLY (to remove)   **GODLY** (to add)

WORLDLY (to remove)　　　　　　　　**GODLY** (to add)

DAY 11

FORGIVE FREELY

DAY 11: FORGIVE FREELY

Today, on DAY 11, we are going to LEARN TO FORGIVE FREELY. This can be a very hard principle to surrender and learn, but it will truly release us from the pain and hurt that keeps us in bondage and weighs us down. We must release it all at the foot of the cross to live in freedom from our bondage and chains.

Luke 23:33-35 says, *"Then they came to the place called The Skull, they crucified Him there, along with the criminals, one on His right and the other on His left. Then Jesus said, 'Father, forgive them, for they know not what they do.' And they divided up His garments by casting lots. The people stood watching as the rulers sneered at Him, saying, 'He saved the others; let Him save Himself if He is the Christ of God, the Chosen One.'"*

How did Jesus do that? And how can we become more like Jesus? He first forgave us, and we are now called to forgive those that trespass against us. We are called to forgive those who hurt us, betrayed us and yes, even crucify us. Jesus is our guide and strength to forgive freely.

Ask God to help you through this journey of forgiveness. It may take many times of prayer and surrender, but action is required. We must speak the words just as Jesus did. This incredible act of forgiveness will free your soul and move you one step closer to fulfilling God's amazing plans in your life.

Colossians 3:13 says, *"Bear with each other and forgive one another if any of you has a grievance against someone. Forgive as the Lord forgave you."* Yes, Jesus forgave us. He sacrificed His life for us. Surely, we can learn to forgive others freely just as Christ did for us. Today, pray for those who you need to forgive, that have hurt you, and pray for those you need forgiveness from.

CHALLENGE: Your journal is divided into three columns. In the first column on the left, write down your offensives and hurts. In the middle column, write who you are going to forgive. And in the third column, write how, or what action, you are going to take to forgive. Actions may include things like calling them or writing a letter, showing them the love of Christ by extending true forgiveness with your sincere words of love, grace and mercy.

Today, on DAY 11 of the Challenge, we choose to FORGIVE FREELY. We choose to ask God to teach us how to forgive and to give us a heart like our Fathers to live in forgiveness for those who betray us, hurt us, and trespass against us.

Ephesians 4:32 says, "*Be kind and compassionate to one another, forgiving each other, just as Christ God forgave you.*"

Surrender it all today and take actions to change your life forever. Be blessed and be a blessing to others today through the act of forgiveness. Your spirit of forgiveness will free yourself and others to live a life in complete freedom and restoration.

SPEND 30 MINUTES IN MEDITATION, PRAYER AND READING HIS WORD. ASK GOD TO REVEAL TO YOU ALL OF THE PAIN AND HURT YOU NEED TO FORGIVE AND ASK HIM FOR GUIDANCE ON THE ACTIONS TO TAKE TO ACHIEVE HIS VICTORIES AND RECEIVE HIS FULLNESS OF BLESSINGS IN YOUR LIFE. WRITE THEM ALL DOWN. FORGIVE THEM ALL.

Watch the encouraging video at www.GodsAmazingPlans.com)

DAY 11: FORGIVE FREELEY

PAIN TO FORGIVE   WHO HURT YOU   ACTION TO TAKE

PAIN TO FORGIVE	WHO HURT YOU	ACTION TO TAKE

PAIN TO FORGIVE	WHO HURT YOU	ACTION TO TAKE

DAY 12

LOVE
UNCONDITIONALLY

DAY 12: LOVE UNCONDITIONALLY

Today is DAY 12 of our Challenge and I celebrate your dedication along your journey and pray for continued strength and perseverance. You will rise up and embrace your amazing plan.

Today on DAY 12, we are going to press into the Lord and begin to learn to let go of all expectations and LOVE UNCONDITIONALLY. We are going to learn to remove our expectations of people to perform for us and to love us a certain way. Luke 6:35 says, *"But love your enemies, and do good and lend, hoping for nothing in return; and your reward shall be great, and ye shall be the children of the Highest; for He is kind unto the unthankful and to the evil."*

Be encouraged that God has gifted us all with a heart of love and as humans we need to be in search of how to love ourselves better, so we can love others better. We will begin our journey of unconditional love like Jesus today, so we can be a light unto this world. In 1 Timothy 1:5, we learn, *"The goal of this command is love, which comes from a pure heart and a good conscience and a sincere faith."* While we didn't meet His expectations, He poured unconditional love on us as we learn in Romans 5:8 *"But God demonstrates His own love for us in this: While we were still sinners, Christ died for us."*

CHALLENGE: Spend time in prayer, meditation and worship today and as you pray, ask Jesus to pour out His power through the Holy Spirit and unconditional love upon you so you can love more like Him. We can learn to love unconditionally when we seek God's heart, wisdom and understanding. He will show us and transform our hearts to love unconditionally like His amazing love for us.

1 John 4:19 says, *"We love because he first loved us."* We must comprehend His unconditional love for us to become more like

Him. You can transform and reflect His image of unconditional love for those around you through the power of His Spirit.

Proverbs 10:12 tells us *"Hatred stirs up strife, but love covers all offenses."* Love, love, love... that is our Godly assignment.

Today, on DAY 12 of the Challenge, we choose to LOVE UNCONDITIONALLY and expect nothing in return. We choose to love because we first loved them and desire to pour out our kind words, kind deeds, precious time, and gifts of provision on them. We choose to love unconditionally with no expectations of them.

We are going to take action today during our prayer time. In the first column, write the NAMES of those people you wish to love unconditionally. In the middle column, write WHAT YOU CAN DO to love them unconditionally. In the third column, write a word that represents unconditional love to you. Use words like free, gift, blessing, just because or whatever words define unconditional, without expectations to you.

Release them today to Abba Father and ask for nothing in return. Seek your Father's heart and ask him to pour out supernatural love on your heart so that you can share it with others.

Be blessed today and be a blessing to others by loving them unconditionally! When people fail you or let you down, show them that their actions are not a condition of your love for them. Bless them abundantly with the unconditional love and power of Jesus.

SPEND 30 MINUTES IN MEDITATION, PRAYER AND READING HIS WORD. ASK GOD TO REVEAL TO YOU NAMES OF THREE PEOPLE YOU HAVE PREVIOUSLY PUT CONDITIONS UPON AND THAT TODAY YOU WOULD LIKE TO BEGIN LOVING UNCONDITIONALLY. WRITE DOWN THE ACTIONS YOU WILL TAKE AND YOUR INSPIRATION FOR LOVING THEM.

(Watch the encouraging video at www.GodsAmazingPlans.com)

DAY 12: LOVE UNCONDITIONALLY

NAMES	ACTION TO TAKE	NO EXPECTATIONS

NAMES	ACTION TO TAKE	NO EXPECTATIONS

DAY 13

EMBRACE YOUR WORTH

DAY 13: EMBRACE YOUR WORTH

Today is DAY 13 of the Challenge and we are going to learn to EMBRACE OUR WORTH. Not our worth in the eyes of this world, but our worth through the eyes and heart of Jesus Christ, our Savior and Creator. We are precious and perfect. We are worthy.

Today, we are going to dig deep in our quiet time to really listen to the words as He describes the person He created. We will open our ears to hear His love for us and how He created us with such worth and value far greater than any rubies or diamonds, silver or gold. Nothing can compare to our worth from Jesus.

In Proverbs 3:13-18, He gives us a glimpse of a wise woman or man when we find the wisdom of who we were created to be. *"Blessed are those who find wisdom, those who gain understanding, for she is more profitable than silver and yields better returns than gold. She is more precious than rubies; nothing you desire can compare with her. Long life is in her right hand; in her left hand are riches and honor. Her ways are pleasant ways, and all her paths are peace. She is a tree of life to those who take hold of her; those who hold her will be blessed."*

That is some worth! Receive that worth today and recognize the love and blessings of your Father to give you that gift of wisdom. Do you want to embrace your worth? Embrace it and proclaim it to your Father for He loves you so much and created you worthy.

He tells us in Psalms 139:13-16, *"For you formed my inward parts; you knitted me together in my mother's womb. I praise you, for I am fearfully and wonderfully made. Wonderful are your works; my soul knows it very well. My frame was not hidden from you, when I was being made in secret, intricately woven in the depths of the earth. Your eyes saw my unformed substance; in your book were written, every one of them, the days that were formed for me, when yet there was none of them."* Let's read Psalms 39:14 again.

126

"I praise you, for I am fearfully and wonderfully made. Wonderful are your works; my soul knows it very well."

Praise you Father for your worth! Help us to embrace our worth every day and to remember who we are in you, Father. Each one of us is valuable to God and to this world. He has created us with an extraordinary purpose, plan and destiny. Embrace your worth!

CHALLENGE: Today, take time to embrace your self-worth as you are created in the image of your Father, including His character. Genesis 1:27 says, *"So God created man in his own image, in the image of God He created him; male and female he created them."*

Today, DAY 13, we choose to EMBRACE OUR WORTH directly from our Father, the Creator of the Heavens and Earth. Isaiah 43:4 says *"Because you are precious in my eyes, and honored, and I love you, I give men in return for you, people in exchange for your life."*

Be blessed today in your Father's loving arms as you recognize your incomparable worth and bless others as you use it wisely.

TODAY, GO BEFORE THE LORD AND PRAY FOR GOD TO REVEAL TO YOU YOUR TRUE WORTH. THEN WRITE A LOVE LETTER FROM A FATHER TO HIS CHILD, AS GOD SPEAKS TO YOU. EMBRACE THE BEAUTIFUL, TALENTED, ANOINTED AND PRECIOUS BEING THAT HE CREATED.

WRITE DOWN EVERYTHING HE REVEALS TO YOU. DO NOT HESITATE ON YOUR JOURNALING. DO NOT EDIT HIS LOVE FOR YOU. DO NOT QUESTION HIS DESCRIPTION OF YOU. LET HIS LOVE FLOW FOR YOU AND LET YOUR WORTH FLOW FROM HIS LIPS TO YOUR HEART. EMBRACE YOUR WORTH AS HE SPEAKS TO YOU.

(Watch the encouraging video on www.GodsAmazingPlans.com)

DAY 13: EMBRACE YOUR WORTH

DEAR PRECIOUS CHILD,

DEAR PRECIOUS CHILD,

DAY 14

PROCLAIM GOD'S GREATNESS

DAY 14: PROCLAIM GOD'S GREATNESS

Today, on DAY 14 of our Challenge, you are going to PROCLAIM GOD'S GREATNESS! You are going to get on a mountaintop and proclaim to the world around you how great your Father is and the amazing things He has done for you because He loves you.

In Psalms 145, we have a good example of praise by David. Let us become proclaimers of God's greatness every day of our lives. *"I will exalt you, my God the King; I will praise your name forever and ever. Every day I will praise you and exalt your name forever and ever. Great is the Lord and most worthy of praise; His greatness no one can fathom. One generation commends your works to another; they tell of your mighty acts. They speak of the glorious splendor of your majesty—and I will meditate on your wonderful works. They tell of the power of your awesome works— and I will proclaim your great deeds. They celebrate your abundant goodness and joyfully sing of your righteousness. The Lord is gracious and compassionate, slow to anger and rich in love. The Lord is good to all; He has compassion on all He has made. All your works praise you, Lord; your faithful people extol you. They tell of the glory of your kingdom and speak of your might, so that all people may know of your mighty acts and the glorious splendor of your kingdom. Your kingdom is an everlasting kingdom, and your dominion endures through all generations. The Lord is trustworthy in all He promises and faithful in all He does. The Lord upholds all who fall and lifts all who are bowed down. The eyes of all look to you, and you give them their food at the proper time. You open your hand and satisfy the desires of every living thing. The Lord is righteous in all His ways and faithful in all He does. The Lord is near to all who call on Him, to all who call on him in truth. He fulfills the desires of those who fear Him; He hears their cry and saves them. The Lord watches over all who love Him, but all the wicked He will destroy. My mouth will speak in praise of the Lord. Let every creature praise His holy name forever and ever."*

CHALLENGE: Today, spend time in prayer and worship, allowing God's Spirit to burn the passion of Christ's love and greatness throughout your body. Feel His passion for His creation and His children and know that He loves you above all things created in this world. We are called and given the authority to rule over all the things of this world. We are appointed to the highest position in all His creation. Take your position and sing out to all who can hear *"How great is our God and all will see how great is our God."*

Deuteronomy 32:3 says, *"I will proclaim the name of the Lord. Oh, praise the greatness of our God!"* Today we will learn to praise Him and proclaim God's greatness to the world. We will learn to proclaim His greatness every day for all to see and hear.

Be blessed and be a blessing to others as you proclaim God's greatness to everyone you encounter. Remind them God is good.

SPEND 30 MINUTES TODAY IN MEDITATION, PRAYER AND READING HIS WORD. THEN PICK UP THE PHONE, TEXT A MESSAGE, WRITE A LETTER OR CARD TO THREE OR MORE PEOPLE THAT GOD ASKS YOU TO PROCLAIM HIS GREATNESS TO. GIVE HIM THANKS FOR THE ASSIGNMENT AND HONOR HIM WITH YOUR PROCLAMATION AND RECOGNITION OF HIS GREATNESS.

(Watch the encouraging video at www.GodsAmazingPlans.com)

DAY 14: PROCLAIM GOD'S GREATNESS

NAMES	ACTION	COMPLETED

NAMES	ACTION	COMPLETED

NAMES	ACTION	COMPLETED

DAY 15

LIVE IN GOD'S PEACE

DAY 15: LIVE IN GOD'S PEACE

Today, on DAY 15 we are going to learn to LIVE IN THE SUPERNATURAL PEACE that surpasses all understanding. Philippians 4:7 tells us *"And the peace of God, which transcends all understanding, will guard your hearts and your minds in Christ Jesus."* This is supernatural peace that guards our hearts and minds. This peace is not of this world and cannot be found in any worldly possessions, desires, or existence. It can only be found in the presence of Christ Jesus.

You will only find this peace through prayer and trusting in His plan for you. Philippians 4:6 says, *"Do not be anxious about anything, but in every situation, by prayer and petition, with thanksgiving, present your requests to God."*

We learn in Exodus 14:14, *"The Lord will fight for you; you need only be still and stand in peace."* Stop fighting, stop looking, stop wondering... you only need to be still in His presence, and you will experience the peace of God's love, protection and provision. Saturate yourself in and with His presence.

He has given you the "shoes of peace" as Apostle Paul speaks about in Ephesians 6. He tells us to stand still and to crush the enemy under your feet, but you must put the shoes on and strap them up to live in readiness and enjoy God's Holy power of peace.

Ephesians 6:15 says, *"And with your feet fitted with the readiness that comes from the gospel of peace."* Peace is a sure sign you are living in God's will and the way He designed you to live. You deserve to live in peace, so let us begin today to live in God's peace from the gospel of truth and wisdom.

Do not worry about the things you cannot control. Depend solely on Him and live in the peace that only He can provide. Psalm

138

29:11 says, *"The Lord gives strength to His people; the Lord blesses His people with peace."* Thank you, Lord!

Romans 5:1 says, *"Therefore, since we have been justified through faith, we have peace with God through our Lord Jesus Christ."* Thank you, Jesus!

CHALLENGE: Today, spend 20 minutes in prayer, worship and meditation. Be still and experience His peace. Ask God to reveal to you three or more things that you are, or have been, worrying about so that you can take direct action to lay them at the cross. Then write them down in your journal.

Give the burden of your worries to Him and live freely in peace. After you identify your worries, visualize holding them in your hand and physically get up, bend over, get to your knees or whatever you can to intentionally lay them at the foot of the cross. Literally lay them down. Let your body, mind, and soul release them to Him. Tell Jesus, here you go... I no longer want to carry these burdens and I trust you will carry them for me. I want to be still and rest in your peace and have faith that you are fighting my battles. I surrender my worries to you in exchange for your peace.

Today, on DAY 15 of the Challenge, we choose to LIVE IN GOD'S PEACE. We choose to lay our burdens down, no longer hold onto worries we cannot control and allow God to defend us in our battles. We choose to rest in His love for us and trust in the promises He gives us about His supernatural peace.

In John 14:27 He promises us, *"Peace I leave with you; my peace I give you. I do not give to you as the world gives. Do not let your hearts be troubled and do not be afraid."*

Say boldly to the world, Not today world! Today, I choose to live in peace. Be blessed today with God's peace and be a blessing to others through His supernatural peace that lives in you.

SPEND 30 MINUTES IN MEDITATION, PRAYER AND READING HIS WORD. ASK GOD TO REVEAL TO YOU ALL BURDENS, WORRIES AND HINDERENCES OF YOUR LIFE. WRITE THEM DOWN AND EXCHANGE THEM WITH GOD FOR HIS SUPERNATURAL PEACE.

(Watch the encouraging video at www.GodsAmazingPlans.com)

DAY 15 LIVE IN GOD'S PEACE

LIST 3 OR MORE BURDENS, WORRIES OR HINDERENCES YOU ARE LAYING DOWN IN EXCHANGE FOR HIS SUPERNATURAL PEACE: (Pray over them)

_____
_____
_____
_____
_____
_____
_____
_____
_____
_____
_____
_____
_____
_____
_____
_____
_____
_____
_____
_____
_____
_____
_____
_____

LIST 3 OR MORE BURDENS, WORRIES OR HINDERENCES YOU ARE LAYING DOWN IN EXCHANGE FOR HIS SUPERNATURAL PEACE: (Pray over them)

_____
_____
_____
_____
_____
_____
_____
_____
_____
_____
_____
_____
_____
_____
_____
_____
_____
_____
_____
_____
_____
_____
_____
_____
_____
_____
_____
_____
_____
_____

LIST 3 OR MORE BURDENS, WORRIES OR HINDERENCES YOU ARE LAYING DOWN IN EXCHANGE FOR HIS SUPERNATURAL PEACE: (Pray over them)

_____
_____
_____
_____
_____
_____
_____
_____
_____
_____
_____
_____
_____
_____
_____
_____
_____
_____
_____
_____
_____
_____
_____
_____
_____
_____
_____
_____
_____

LIST 3 OR MORE BURDENS, WORRIES OR HINDERENCES YOU ARE LAYING DOWN IN EXCHANGE FOR HIS SUPERNATURAL PEACE: (Pray over them)

DAY 16

BE
THANKFUL

DAY 16: BE THANKFUL

Today is DAY 16 of the Challenge. We are half way through our Challenge and hopefully you are feeling closer to God; closer to living out His amazing plans in your life. Today, we are going to learn to live in His will and BE THANKFUL children of God.

1 Chronicles 29:13 says, *"And now we thank you, our God, and praise your glorious name."* and in Ephesians 5:20 we learn to *"Give thanks in all circumstances; for this is the will of God in Christ Jesus for you."* So, let us be thankful.

Psalm 118:2 says *"You are my God, and I will give thanks to you; you are my God; I will extol you."* Yes Jesus, we are thankful, and we will be thankful and show our gratitude for your amazing love and grace. In 2 Corinthians 9:15, Paul teaches us that we have been given an inexpressible gift. *"Thanks be to God for His inexpressible gift!"* Thank Him for His inexpressible gift to you.

It is so important to develop the spirit of thankfulness and learn to live our lives with a thankful heart. Philippians 4:6 says, *"Petition the Lord with a thankful heart"* Thankfulness is the key to unlocking the power of miracles through prayer. If you have the key in your hand and heart to unlock the abundance of God's blessings and favor, wouldn't you use it wisely? Start today to always be thankful and watch how God starts changing your life and starts revealing your amazing plans.

God designed us to be thankful people, but we often let the world steal and kill our joy. We lose focus of what is good that we have and instead focus on what we don't have. But today we will refocus our eyes on what is good and what we do have. We will focus on Jesus today and everyday as we keep our eyes fixed on Him and we learn to be thankful for His inexpressible gift.

Ephesians 5:20 tells us that *"Giving thanks always and for everything to God the Father in the name of our Lord Jesus Christ."*

Let us learn to be thankful always and in everything. Focus on the good and give no worth to the bad. The supernatural good will begin to grow and the bad will begin to diminish before our very eyes. It is supernatural through the Spirit of God.

Psalm 30:12 says, *"That my glory may sing your praise and not be silent. O' Lord my God, I will give thanks to you forever!"*

1 Thessalonians 5:18 instructs us, *"Give thanks in all circumstances; for this is God's will for you in Christ Jesus."* If you want to truly live in God's will and walk on God's path and not your own, then surrender your heart to Jesus and begin to be thankful in all circumstances and learn to be grateful forever. Be thankful every day for something in your life. Count it all as joy my friend.

CHALLENGE: Today, as you pray, thank Him for everything you have, everything you are, and everything he has done for you. Leave nothing out. BE THANKFUL for everything in your life. Write a list of as many things as you can that you are thankful for; even life's challenges. For in the challenges there are lessons and beauty often beyond what we as humans can see. I challenge you to fill a whole page with gratitude and watch the supernatural transform your heart from worry to faith and emptiness to fullness.

Today, on DAY 16 of the Challenge, we choose to be thankful to our Heavenly Father, the Creator of the Heavens and Earth. Thankful for our life. Thankful for our health. Thankful for our salvation. Thankful for our family. Thankful for His provision. Thankful for His forgiveness. Thankful for... EVERYTHING!

Count your blessings today and be a blessing to others with an attitude of gratitude as they watch you be thankful for all things in your life. Your gratitude for life is an example for others to follow.

SPEND 30 MINUTES IN MEDITATION, PRAYER AND READING HIS WORD. THANK GOD OPENLY AND OFTEN FOR ALL OF THE BLESSINGS AND CIRCUMSTANCES OF YOUR LIFE. IN YOUR JOURNAL, WRITE YOUR LETTER OF THANKFULNESS TO GOD.

(Watch the encouraging video at www.GodsAmazingPlans.com)

DAY 16: BE THANKFUL

DEAR HEAVENLY FATHER, I AM THANKFUL FOR:

_____
_____
_____
_____
_____
_____
_____
_____
_____
_____
_____
_____
_____
_____
_____
_____
_____
_____
_____
_____
_____

DEAR HEAVENLY FATHER, I AM THANKFUL FOR:

DEAR HEAVENLY FATHER, I AM THANKFUL FOR:

DEAR HEAVENLY FATHER, I AM THANKFUL FOR:

DAY 17

REST
IN
JESUS

DAY 17: REST IN JESUS

Today is DAY 17 of the Challenge and we are going to learn to REST IN JESUS. It says in Matthew 11:28, *"Come to me, all you who are weary and burdened, and I will give you rest."* Another version says Jesus tells us, *"Come be with me by yourself to a quiet place because you need rest."* We all need rest and Jesus knew we would; so, enjoy your time today learning to rest in Jesus. Rest in His presence where the supernatural rest exists.

Take a break right now from the worries of the day and rest in Jesus today. No, seriously, take a moment and ponder what resting in Jesus's arms would really feel like. Then, rest in your Abba Father's arms just as you imagined. Completely let yourself melt into Him and let Him restore your soul. He goes before you to prepare your way. When you slow down and rest in Him, trust that while you rest, He is fighting your battles and preparing your way.

Rest requires surrendering control and letting Him fight your battles, allowing Him to remove all obstacles from your path that weigh you down and divert you from your amazing plan and destiny. When we don't learn spiritual rest, we struggle and try to fight our battles on our own, which leads to exhaustion and frustration.

Psalm 37:7 tells us to *"Rest in the LORD and wait patiently for Him; Do not fret because of him who prospers in his way, Because of the man who carries out wicked schemes."*

Stop fighting, stop exhausting yourself and start learning to REST IN JESUS for strength, comfort, direction, guidance, restoration and resolution. He is waiting for you. We must learn to be still. In Psalms 46:10 He says, *"Be still and know that I am God."* Don't be distracted by busyness. Start learning to REST IN JESUS. Learn to be still and rest in the wisdom that He is good and faithful.

154

CHALLENGE: After prayer and resting in the Lord's arms today, write down all the things you experienced: senses, sounds, emotions, and tangible feelings; physical, mental, emotional and spiritual encounters in His arms and in His Holy presence.
Then I want you to meditate on His Spirit and ask Him to reveal to you all the things that are making you weary and burdened. What are the things that are making you tired? We need to know them and be aware that they are disconnecting you from the Spirit of God. We may not be able to remove all of them, but we can become aware of them, so we can lay them daily at the cross.

Today, on DAY 17 of the Challenge, we choose to rest in Jesus as He instructed us. We choose to recognize that He created us for rest and that He is our only source for true rest in this world of busyness and distractions. We choose to recharge daily in His presence and rest in His arms. We choose to rest in Jesus.

Be blessed today and be a blessing to others by sharing the secret to restoration and refreshing of the soul by resting in Jesus.

SPEND 30 MINUTES IN MEDITATION, PRAYER AND RESTING IN JESUS. IN YOUR JOURNAL, WRITE DOWN WHAT RESTING IN JESUS LOOKED LIKE FOR YOU AS YOU MEDITATED. THEN WRITE THE THINGS THAT ARE MAKING YOU WEARY AND TIRED. PRAY OVER THEM AND LAY THEM AT THE CROSS. LEARN TO DO THIS DAILY AND CHANGE YOUR LIFE,

(Watch the encouraging video at www.GodsAmazingPlans.com)

DAY 17: REST IN JESUS

RESTING IN JESUS FOR ME LOOKS LIKE:

_____

_____

_____

_____

RESTING IN JESUS FOR ME LOOKS LIKE:

WRITE THE THINGS THAT ARE MAKING YOU WEARY AND TIRED. LAY THEM AT THE FEET OF JESUS AND REST.

WRITE THE THINGS THAT ARE MAKING YOU WEARY AND TIRED. LAY THEM AT THE FEET OF JESUS AND REST.

_____
_____
_____
_____
_____
_____
_____
_____
_____
_____
_____
_____
_____
_____
_____
_____
_____
_____
_____
_____
_____
_____
_____
_____
_____
_____
_____
_____
_____
_____

WRITE THE THINGS THAT ARE MAKING YOU WEARY AND TIRED. LAY THEM AT THE FEET OF JESUS AND REST.

_____
_____
_____
_____
_____
_____
_____
_____
_____
_____
_____
_____
_____
_____
_____
_____
_____
_____
_____
_____
_____
_____
_____
_____
_____
_____
_____
_____
_____
_____
_____

DAY 18

COMPETE
WITH
NO ONE

DAY 18: COMPETE WITH NO ONE

Today is DAY 18 of our Challenge and it is a very important one for your personal growth and maturity as you walk into God's amazing plans for your life. Today, we are going to learn to COMPETE WITH NO ONE!

God created you with a unique plan and destiny. He gave you the perfect personality, talents, and skills necessary to fulfill that destiny. The Bible tells us that we are all born with distinct talents and gifts that set us apart from each other. When you discover the talents that God has given you and you use them to glorify Him, you will experience a full life and step into your destiny.

Our loving Lord wants us to feel whole and complete, and it is through our talents that we can find our unique calling in life. Today, we are going to learn about our God-given talents to encourage ourselves, and learn not to compete with others, but rather to use our talents to help others live out their amazing plans, too. We choose to partner and not compete with others, but to become stronger by developing allies to achieve God's work.

1 Corinthians 12:5-6 tells us, *"There are different kinds of service, but the same Lord. There are different kinds of working, but in all of them and in everyone it is the same God at work."*

1 Peter 4:10 says, *"Each of you should use whatever gift you have received to serve others, as faithful stewards of God's grace in its various forms."*

God has a plan for everyone and we are all individual members contributing to the body of Christ. Each of our gifts work together to build the Kingdom of God. You are a masterpiece and as you mature and grow as a Christian, you will begin to truly see how special and unique God created you. We learned from David, as he shared in Psalms 139:13-14, *"You alone created my inner being. You knitted me together inside my mother. I will give thanks to you because I have been so amazingly and miraculously made. Your works are miraculous, and my soul is fully aware of this."* Amen!

You are amazing just the way you are. You don't have to keep waiting, you must begin believing and understanding that He prepared you in advance. You are ready!   No more competing. No more wishing you had something more or didn't have certain God given qualities or characteristics. No more comparing. No more thinking you don't have enough or are not quite ready.

You are ready! God is waiting for you to step into your destiny and compete with no one. Just be the person He created you to be. It's that simple. Once you learn this, you will begin stepping into His plan, running your race and competing with no one.

Isaiah 64:8 says, *"Yet you, Lord, are our Father. We are the clay, you are the potter; we are all the work of your hand."* Let your Father mold you and shape you as you press into Him and seek His direction and counsel. He can and will mold and shape you.

Note: you are only part of the plan. Others will help you fulfill your destiny, just as you are going to help others step into theirs. This journey is not meant to walk alone, nor is it meant to compete against one another. Rather, we are created as parts to make a whole, as we learn in 1 Corinthians 12:20, *"As it is, there are many parts, but one body."* Your part is critical in HIS PLAN for your life, but also for His Kingdom Plan.

CHALLENGE: Today, I encourage you to spend time in prayer with Abba Father and ask Him to reveal to you the people around you as your allies and partners, not as your competitors or challengers.

Write in your journal the names of three people you compare yourself to, and perhaps even as a competitor. Then, beside their

163

names, write PARTNER. When we change our heart and mind, we understand God's will and God's ways. Let God help you see them as your partners, helping you fulfill your God given destiny. Today, thank them for being part of your life journey and recognize them as a valuable partner in your amazing plan.

Today, on DAY 18 of our journey to live out God's amazing plan, we choose to COMPETE WITH NO ONE; to be the fabulous YOU that God created you to be.

We choose to recognize that our gifts were created just for us, and that by competing with others, we are not using our gifts as God intended. We choose to no longer watch others and compare ourselves as we are running our race, but rather we choose to stay in our own lanes and run the race God has set before us. We choose to live our life as God designed.

We choose to be happy for other's success, gifts and ways that God is using them to build the Kingdom of God and glorify His name. We choose to celebrate those around us that are thriving.

Be blessed and be a blessing to others by not competing with them, but by lifting them up and helping them rise to their calling and live out their amazing plan.

SPEND 30 MINUTES IN MEDITATION, PRAYER AND READING HIS WORD. ASK GOD TO REVEAL TO YOU THE PEOPLE YOU COMPETE WITH AND INSTEAD BEGIN TO PRAY FOR WAYS YOU CAN PARTNER WITH THEM. WRITE THEM ALL DOWN.

(Watch the encouraging video at www.GodsAmazingPlans.com)

DAY 18: COMPETE WITH NO ONE

LIST 3 PEOPLE YOU CURRENTLY COMPARE YOURSELF TO OR EVEN COMPETE WITH:

LIST 3 PEOPLE YOU CURRENTLY COMPARE YOURSELF TO OR EVEN COMPETE WITH:

1._____
_____
_____

2._____
_____
_____

3._____
_____
_____

DEAR LORD, I SURRENDER THESE COMPARISONS AND WANT TO BE USED BY YOU AS PERFECTLY DESIGNED:

_____
_____
_____
_____
_____
_____
_____
_____
_____
_____
_____
_____
_____
_____
_____

DEAR LORD, I SURRENDER THESE COMPARISONS AND WANT TO BE USED BY YOU AS PERFECTLY DESIGNED:

DEAR LORD, I SURRENDER THESE COMPARISONS AND WANT TO BE USED BY YOU AS PERFECTLY DESIGNED:

DAY 19

DO NOT FOLLOW MAN, ONLY FOLLOW GOD

DAY 19: DO NOT FOLLOW MAN, ONLY FOLLOW GOD

Today is DAY 19 of our Challenge and we are going to learn to FOLLOW ONLY GOD; NOT MAN. Man can lead us to destruction, but God will never lead us astray. Make sure to keep your eyes and ears open to recognize the voices you are following.

Acts 5:29 tells us, "Peter and the other apostles replied: '*We must obey God rather than human beings!*'" That's a simple statement, but can we follow it daily? Today, we will begin to search our Father's heart and ask for His help to follow only God, not man.

Following God begins with spending intimate time with Him daily; which is why you chose to do this Challenge and create a habit that will lead you to His amazing plans for you. John 10:4 says "*When He has brought out all His own, He goes on ahead of them, and His sheep follow Him because they know His voice.*"

In Leviticus 18:44 we learn from God, "*You must obey my laws and be careful to follow my decrees. I am the LORD your God.*" He is instructing us to be careful not to follow man, but rather to follow Him. He is guiding us to His great plan and purpose for our life.

Matthew 16:24 reads, "*Then Jesus said to His disciples, 'Whoever wants to be my disciple must deny themselves and take up their cross and follow me.'*" We must carry our cross daily to remind us of His plan for us—a guideline on how to live our lives through His strength, with His guidance, and by His Spirit.

Those who listened to the voice of Jesus in the New Testament and those of us who listen to Him now, get to choose between following the light of the Lord or walking in the darkness of the world. We have a decision to make—one will give us life, hope and joy in our lives—the other will lead to pain, suffering, and difficulties. Jesus is the only one that offers us a love relationship and an abundant life by FOLLOWING GOD, NOT MAN.

"Follow only God" are three words that sound easy but can be very difficult to carry out. In 1 John 4:8, the Bible states *"God is love,"* so when we follow the way of love we choose God's laws and God's ways. Jesus led by example, and He lived out loud the law that was given to Him by His Father. By learning to follow only God, not man, we can begin to develop a relationship with the source of love, truth, comfort, and peace. Following only God will bring us indescribable joy, blessings, and "life" that comes from going where God leads us. Our lives are full of choices, so what decision will you make today? Will you follow man? Or will you choose to follow only God?

Galatians 1:10 asks, *"Am I now trying to win the approval of human beings, or of God? Or am I trying to please people? If I were still trying to please people, I would not be a servant of Christ."*

CHALLENGE: Today, after prayer, I want you to list out the three most important priorities in your life and check them against God's plan for your life. Spend time in prayer and ask God to reveal the truth about your motivations and agendas behind your identified desires and goals. If they are created by man, for man or you are unsure, release them at the foot of the cross during prayer and ask God to help you follow only Him. Surrender yourself to God.

Today, on DAY 19 of our Challenge, we choose to follow only God and no longer follow man. John 8:12 states, *"When Jesus spoke again to the people, He said, 'I am the light of the world. Whoever follows me will never walk in darkness but will have the light of life."*

Today, we choose to live in the light and no longer walk in darkness. We choose to seek God for wisdom and direction. We choose to seek the counsel of God before we seek the counsel of men. We choose to always go to prayer and stand before our Father as we are faced with decisions, choices and challenges.

Our Father is the one who created us; He is the only one who knows His plans for our life and is the only one working out all things for our good in our lives. Choose to follow God, not man.

Be blessed and be a blessing to others by pointing them to the only source for answers to their questions and decisions when they ask you for advice. Direct them to follow God, not man.

SPEND 30 MINUTES IN MEDITATION, PRAYER AND READING HIS WORD. ASK GOD FOR STRENGTH, WISDOM AND INSIGHT TO FOLLOW HIS PLANS FOR YOUR LIFE AND NOT YOUR OWN. WRITE DOWN YOUR MOST IMPORTANT PRIORITIES IN LIFE AND ASK HIM TO HELP YOU IDENTIFY WHETHER THESE ARE OF HIM OR OF MAN.

(Watch the encouraging video at www.GodsAmazingPlans.com)

DAY 19 DO NOT FOLLOW MAN, ONLY FOLLOW GOD

MOST IMPORTANT ROLES AND GOALS	ARE THEY OF/FOR GOD? EXPLAIN HOW

MOST IMPORTANT ROLES AND GOALS	ARE THEY OF/FOR GOD? EXPLAIN HOW

MOST IMPORTANT ROLES AND GOALS	ARE THEY OF/FOR GOD? EXPLAIN HOW

MOST IMPORTANT ROLES AND GOALS	ARE THEY OF/FOR GOD? EXPLAIN HOW

PRAY, SEARCH YOUR HEART, REFLECT AND EXPOSE FEAR:

FEAR OF MAN'S REJECTION   FEAR OF GOD'S REJECTION

PRAY, SEARCH YOUR HEART, REFLECT AND EXPOSE FEAR:

FEAR OF MAN'S REJECTION   FEAR OF GOD'S REJECTION

DAY 20

LET GOD DIRECT YOUR STEPS

DAY 20: LET GOD DIRECT YOUR STEPS

Congratulations! You have made it to DAY 20, which is two-thirds of the way through the Challenge. I am so excited for you and what God has been doing in your life, revealing to you as you commit to spending time with Him. He will continue to reveal more over the next 10 days as you complete this Challenge.

Today, on DAY 20 of our Challenge, we are going to learn to LET GOD DIRECT OUR STEPS.

Proverbs 3:5-6 says, *"Trust in the Lord with all your heart; and lean not unto your own understanding. In all your ways, submit to Him, and He will make your paths straight."*

How many of you would like to walk a straight path to your destiny as opposed to a windy, curvy, bumpy path that takes you in circles around and around the mountain? In this verse, God tells us when we trust Him and submit to His ways, He directs our steps along a straight path.

I often hear God remind me that His straight path takes less time, less effort, and that it is an easier road. Most importantly, He says that it is His path and His plan for my life. He gently reminds me of the plan He originally created for Adam and Eve, if only they would have trusted and submitted to Him.

Today's Challenge is to let GOD DIRECT YOUR STEPS along His amazing path for you. He knows the plan and so, of course, He knows the way and which steps are best to take along the path. When we can trust Him and submit to His ways, I only have one thing to say: I am warning you to watch out, because when you start doing life God's way, you better get ready to be ready!

Supernatural things start happening only by the power of God. Doors start opening, obstacles start disappearing, miracles start occurring, and your path becomes straighter, just as promised. You will know these things are of God because they will be far greater than anything you are capable of on your own. You will have no choice but to depend on God and stop relying on your own strength and desires. One step on God's path leads to another step on His path which leads to another step in His will.

Proverbs 16:9 says, *"In their hearts, humans plan their course, but the LORD establishes their steps."*

CHALLENGE: Today, I want you to go before the Lord and pray for the path to be lit upon your feet, just like His word tells us in Psalms 119:105, *"Your word is a lamp for my feet, a light on my path."*

Pray for a light so bright on your path that you cannot miss it. Pray for His voice to be so clear and loud that you cannot miss it. Pray for a stone path to appear from the ground that will clearly lead to His amazing plan for your life. Pray for God to reveal a path like the one in my life that I shared with you on today's challenge encouraging video.

Today, tell God that you will follow Him in complete obedience wherever the path may lead. Tell God that you are ready to follow His steps and that you trust they will lead to your destiny.

In Luke 9:57, as they were walking along the road, a man said to him, *"I will follow you wherever you go."* ... and in Luke 9:61-62, another said, *"I will follow You, Lord; but first let me bid farewell to my family."* Then Jesus declared, *"No one who puts his hand to the plow and then looks back is fit for the kingdom of God."* Jesus is saying, if you have heard me, direct your steps, be obedient and don't hesitate, wonder or doubt. Trust Him, and submit your ways to Him, and He will make your path straight.

Be blessed and be a blessing to others as you let God direct your steps and walk along His path to your amazing plan.

AS YOU PRAY TODAY AND ASK FOR YOUR PATH TO BE LIT,

WRITE DOWN THE STEPS HE IS REVEALING FOR YOU TO TAKE ALONG THE JOURNEY. WRITE DOWN EVERY STEP, EVERY WORD, AND EVERY VISION HE GIVES YOU. THEN PRAY OVER THEM DAILY AND ASK HIM TO PROMPT YOU WHEN IT IS TIME TO TAKE EACH STEP.

SURRENDER YOUR PLANS TO HIM AND BE READY TO BE IN AWE OF THE DOORS HE WILL OPEN, THE PLACES YOU WILL GO AND THE THINGS THAT YOU WILL ACCOMPLISH. YOU ARE LEARNING TO WALK ON HIS PATH, AND NOT YOUR OWN.

(Watch the encouraging video at www.GodsAmazingPlans.com)

DAY 20: LET GOD DIRECT YOUR STEPS

LIST THE STEPS AND PLANS GOD REVEALED TO YOU:

_____
_____
_____
_____
_____
_____
_____
_____
_____
_____
_____
_____
_____
_____
_____
_____
_____
_____
_____

LIST THE STEPS AND PLANS GOD REVEALED TO YOU:

_____
_____
_____
_____
_____
_____
_____
_____
_____
_____
_____
_____
_____
_____
_____
_____
_____
_____
_____
_____
_____
_____
_____
_____
_____
_____
_____
_____
_____
_____
_____
_____

LIST THE STEPS AND PLANS GOD REVEALED TO YOU:

_____
_____
_____
_____
_____
_____
_____
_____
_____
_____
_____
_____
_____
_____
_____
_____
_____
_____
_____
_____
_____
_____
_____
_____
_____
_____
_____
_____
_____
_____

LIST THE STEPS AND PLANS GOD REVEALED TO YOU:

_____

_____

_____

_____

_____

_____

_____

_____

_____

_____

_____

_____

_____

_____

_____

_____

_____

_____

_____

_____

_____

_____

_____

_____

_____

_____

_____

_____

_____

_____

DAY 21

HAVE
UNSHAKABLE
FAITH
IN GOD

DAY 21: HAVE UNSHAKABLE FAITH IN GOD

Today is DAY 21 of our Challenge and we are going to learn to HAVE UNSHAKABLE FAITH IN GOD. We are going to take it a step further than simply saying we have faith, we are going to take action and step into unshakable faith. Faith requires action.

In 1 Samuel 17:45, David said to the Philistine, *"You come against me with sword and spear and javelin, but I come against you in the name of the LORD Almighty, the God of the armies of Israel, whom you have defied."*

David had faith in God and he acted because he knew the power and promises of His God. He took action with his faith. He used the smallest of human weapons; one stone, and the most powerful spiritual weapon; unshakable faith. He acted against the mighty warrior, Goliath, and won because of his unshakable faith in His powerful and mighty God.

In Matthew 14:27-32, we learn the power of what can happen when we keep our eyes on God as we learn to have faith and take action. Jesus said to them: *"Take courage! It is I. Do not be afraid." "Lord, if it is you," Peter replied, "Tell me to come to you on the water." "Come," He said." Then Peter got out of the boat, walked on the water and came toward Jesus. But when he saw the wind, he was afraid and, beginning to sink, cried out, "Lord, save me!" Immediately Jesus reached out His hand and caught him. "You of little faith," He said, "Why did you doubt?" And when they climbed into the boat, the wind died down."*

This is a very important lesson as we step out in faith. We cannot let the distractions of this world and our trials overcome our faith in God. Doubt and fear are faith killers. We are going to learn to conquer doubt and fear through today's Challenge.

Faith and fear cannot exist in our mind or heart if we are to truly live out God's amazing plans. Remember Jesus being tempted by

188

the devil? It was Jesus's faith in His Father's word and truth that allowed Him not to be fooled by temptation or the empty and false promises of greatness outside of God's plan. The devil is going to try to tempt you, too. He wants to shake your faith in God and distract you from achieving your powerful purpose. You become bold in your faith when you know God's truth and Spirit as Jesus, Peter and David did.

I love how simply Jesus states it here to His disciples in Mark 11:22, *"Have faith in God,"* Jesus answered. He goes on to tell them, and us, something very important about doubt and fear in our acts of faith through Mark 11:23-25. Jesus said, *"Truly I tell you, if anyone says to this mountain, 'Go, throw yourself into the sea,' and does not doubt in their heart but believes that what they say will happen, it will be done for them. Therefore, I tell you, whatever you ask for in prayer, believe that you have received it, and it will be yours. And when you stand praying, if you hold anything against anyone, forgive them, so that your Father in heaven may forgive you of your sins."*

I tell you, don't ask for it if you don't want to believe it. But if you are ready to receive what God has planned for you, then ask without any doubt of who you are, how valuable you are, how precious you are, and how important you are in the plan that God has created for you and for His Kingdom purposes.

We must also learn that faith in God requires faith in His timing. Habakkuk 2:2-3 says, *"Write it clearly on tablets, so that anyone who reads it may run. For the vision points ahead to a time I have appointed; it testifies regarding the end, and it will not lie. Even if there is a delay, wait for it."*

We must have faith in God, which includes His power, His promises, His love for us and His timing. He knows His plans and purposes for all things in our lives. We must learn to have faith in God and trust in His timing.

Today, we are going to take a step of faith and trust in our Lord wholeheartedly, with our deepest needs and dreams.

We are going to move the mountains before us by believing in who our Father is. The Bible tells us we need only have the faith of a mustard seed. I am convinced, it is not the size, but it is the heartfelt trust we put in our God, and the removal of fear and doubt from our lives that will enable us to move the mountains blocking our path to live out His amazing plans. Let's explore faith through action.

CHALLENGE: Today, go into prayer with your Father and ask Him to reveal to you at least three things He is calling for you to have faith in Him. Find at least three obstacles or challenges that you are facing, like David facing Goliath, where you need God's guidance, support, strength and wisdom. Write them down in your journal. Then lay your hand over them and ask God to give you the strength, courage and bold faith in God to conquer any fear or doubt. Write down anything God reveals to you about unshakable faith. Hold on to them through the storms, like Peter, and remember to keep your eyes fixed on God.

Today, on DAY 21 of our Challenge, we choose to HAVE UNSHAKABLE FAITH IN GOD, like David and Peter. We choose to not be afraid of what we cannot see or know. We choose to trust in His timing. We choose to have unshakable faith in God in all circumstances of life like Jesus.

Be blessed and be a blessing to others as they watch your unshakable faith in God grow, and lived out in your actions, as you face the persecution of enemies and the destructive storms of life.

PRAY, MEDITATE AND ASK GOD TO REVEAL TO YOU THE MOUNTAINS THAT ARE STANDING BEFORE YOU. PRAY OVER THESE OFTEN AND WATCH YOUR FAITH TAKE ACTION AND YOUR FEARS DECREASE. THEN WRITE WHAT GOD INSTRUCTS YOU TO DO TO HAVE UNSHAKABLE FAITH.

(Watch the encouraging video at www.GodsAmazingPlans.com)

DAY 21: HAVE FAITH IN GOD

LIST THE 3 OR MORE THINGS GOD WANTS YOU TO HAVE FAITH IN HIM FOR:

1._____
_____
_____
_____
_____
_____
_____
_____

2._____
_____
_____
_____
_____
_____
_____
_____

3._____
_____
_____
_____
_____
_____
_____
_____

LIST THE 3 OR MORE THINGS GOD WANTS YOU TO HAVE FAITH IN HIM FOR:

1._____
_____
_____
_____
_____
_____
_____

2._____
_____
_____
_____
_____
_____
_____

3._____
_____
_____
_____
_____
_____
_____
_____
_____

GOD REVEALED TO ME THESE THINGS I NEED TO DO TO HAVE UNSHAKABLE FAITH:

GOD REVEALED TO ME THESE THINGS I NEED TO DO TO HAVE UNSHAKABLE FAITH:

_____
_____
_____
_____
_____
_____
_____
_____
_____
_____
_____
_____
_____
_____
_____
_____
_____
_____
_____
_____
_____
_____
_____
_____
_____
_____
_____
_____
_____
_____
_____
_____
_____
_____

GOD REVEALED TO ME THESE THINGS I NEED TO DO TO HAVE UNSHAKABLE FAITH:

DAY 22

TRUST
WHOLE
HEARTEDLY
IN GOD

DAY 22: TRUST WHOLEHEARTEDLY IN GOD

Today is DAY 22 of our Challenge, and today we are going to learn to TRUST WHOLEHEARTEDLY IN THE LORD; not only when it feels good and life is easy, but also when things are difficult, and life is a challenge.

Proverbs 3:5 says, *"Trust in the LORD with all your heart and lean not on your own understanding;"* This means, trust in Him with all your heart, not just some of your heart on some days, but all of your heart and through every day and every circumstance.

It only takes a mustard seed of faith to trust, but it must be with your whole heart. Trust is when we can't see it, but we know it is for sure. In 2 Corinthians 5:7 we are called to *"walk by faith, not by sight."* We can learn to trust wholeheartedly, without a shadow of a doubt and know that all things will work together for our good when we love the Lord; even when we are in the storms of life.

In Numbers 14:24, we learn about Caleb's trust in the Lord, *"But because my servant Caleb has a different spirit and follows Me wholeheartedly, I will bring him into the land he went to, and his descendants will inherit it."* During tragedy, Caleb stood out as a hero. Why? He had what the Bible calls "a different spirit" or attitude. He followed and trusted God wholeheartedly.

What does it mean to follow God wholeheartedly? Caleb trusted God and refused to rebel against Him. These two traits cause people to stand out from the crowd. When we trust God, despite evidence to the contrary, we will stand out. Others will doubt, complain, and make excuses. But if you continue to trust God when times are tough, and you choose not to doubt, complain or make excuses, others will notice. And so, will God.

Second, Caleb refused to rebel against the Lord. There is a saying that when times are tough, the tough get tougher. But I would encourage you when times get tough, the tough should trust wholeheartedly in the Lord. We may not have the strength to move forward when life is falling apart, but we can learn to trust that God has us at our current destination for purpose, so we must refuse to retreat, and we must decide to trust wholeheartedly in God.

Caleb was a man with a different spirit: he trusted God wholeheartedly. Today, we are going to search our own hearts and ask God to remove those things that we are not trusting Him with wholeheartedly and ask Him to give us a spirit like Caleb's.

CHALLENGE: Today, pray about the desires of your heart, the fears you experience in life, the challenges you face with friends and family that you are not trusting wholeheartedly with God. These could be simple things or difficult things. They could be bitterness and negativity, or rebellion and disobedience. Write them all in your journal. Write them all as you confess them to the Lord.

Then, I want you to imagine holding them in your hand and offer them to God. Ask Him to remove them from your hand and wait for God to remove them from you. Then pray again and wait upon the Lord as you ask Him to replace your distrust with wholehearted trust about these circumstances.

Ask Him to lay in your hand a word, an item, a vision, or a confirmation of His removal of the distrust and the replacement of His new gift of wholehearted trust. Wait until He replaces the old with something new. He is faithful, and you can trust Him wholeheartedly. He will remove your fear and replace it with faith.

Trust in Him wholeheartedly as you wait for His gift. Write down your experience of this exchange. Write down what you gave Him and what He gave you in return. Write it all down as evidence that God is watching you, hearing you, and is with you.

This journey is about evidence that God is real and that through our faith and His presence, He will transform us and reveal to us His amazing plans for our lives. Our plans will begin to unfold before our very eyes as we seek Him and trust wholeheartedly in Him.

Today, on DAY 22 of our journey, we choose to TRUST IN GOD WHOLEHEARTEDLY. We choose to have a Spirit like Caleb during hardship. We choose to live our life with a different spirit or attitude than others around us. We choose to stand out for God and to be a light in this world, or like Caleb a "hero" to others who see us and know us. We choose to trust in God wholeheartedly every single day, under every single circumstance.

Be blessed and be a blessing to others today with a different spirit like Caleb. Be somebody's "hero" today as you display trust in God wholeheartedly.

SPEND 30 MINUTES IN MEDITATION, PRAYER AND READING HIS WORD. ASK GOD TO REVEAL TO YOU ALL AREAS IN YOUR LIFE THAT YOU ARE NOT TRUSTING HIM. THEN HAND TO GOD YOUR FEAR AND EXCHANGE IT FOR HIS GIFT AND LEARN HOW TO TRUST HIM MORE. WRITE IT DOWN.

(Watch the encouraging video at www.GodsAmazingPlans.com)

DAY 22: TRUST WHOLEHEARTEDLY IN GOD

THINGS NOT TRUSTING GOD:	**GOD'S REPLACEMENT:**
(Negative/Bitter/Doubt/Fear)	(His exchange of goodness)

THINGS NOT TRUSTING GOD:

(Negative/Bitter/Doubt/Fear)

GOD'S REPLACEMENT:

(His exchange of goodness)

THINGS NOT TRUSTING GOD:

(Negative/Bitter/Doubt/Fear)

GOD'S REPLACEMENT:

(His exchange of goodness)

THINGS NOT TRUSTING GOD:

(Negative/Bitter/Doubt/Fear)

GOD'S REPLACEMENT:

(His exchange of goodness)

DAY 23

HAVE AN
ATTITUDE
OF
GRATITUDE

DAY 23: HAVE AN ATTITUDE OF GRATITUDE

Today is DAY 23 of our Challenge. Only 7 more days and you did it! 30 days conquered, and you are closer to living in God's will and wiser to His amazing plan for your life.

Today we are going to learn TO HAVE AN ATTITUDE OF GRATITUDE. We are going to become a person that lives in gratitude the way God designed us. He wants us to focus on Him and what He has created in us. He created so much for us and has given us so much to be thankful for, so today, we will begin to recognize, embrace and appreciate everything!

Colossians 3:16-17 tells us, *"Let the message of Christ dwell among you richly as you teach and admonish one another with all wisdom through psalms, hymns, and songs from the Spirit, singing to God with gratitude in the name of the Lord Jesus, giving thanks to God the Father through him."* Today, we will change any of our stinking thinking to an attitude of gratitude.

Colossians 4:2 tells us to simply, *"Devote yourselves to prayer, being watchful and thankful."* Let us begin in prayer today and ask God to help us be watchful and thankful for all we have.

In Psalms 50:14 God tells us, *"I am God most high! The only sacrifice I want is for you to be thankful and for you to keep your word."* Let us become thankful people and glorify our God by living our lives with an attitude of gratitude in all circumstances.

An attitude of gratitude keeps us obedient to God, avoiding anything that grieves Him. Ezra 10:11 tells us, *"Now honor the Lord, the God of your ancestors, and do His will. Separate yourselves from the peoples around you."*

Can you become obedient to the Lord and glorify Him with your life and your attitude of thanksgiving? Honor Him with an attitude of gratitude and separate yourselves from the people around you. Ask yourself this question everyday: *What if today you woke up with only the things you thanked God for yesterday?* Wow! What would you have in your life today if this question was true?

Today we want to begin to get in the mindset and habit of thanking Him every day for everything you want to still have tomorrow. I want you to take time to list, and then personally thank God for all the blessings of your life. Taking an account for what we have and the things that are going right in our life can help to outweigh the negatives and burdens that life can throw at us and knock us off course of our amazing plans. I encourage you to do this daily.

CHALLENGE: Spend time in prayer, meditation and worship with your Abba Father asking Him to reveal to you how to honor Him and to recognize all the things you are grateful for in your life. Then in your journal, write down at least 20 or more blessings, gifts, or good things going on in your life. Don't focus on the challenges, only the things that bless you.

Do not allow yourself to be distracted by negatives or challenges. Focus your attention on having an attitude of gratitude. If you have more than 20, keep writing. When you express gratitude, you are honoring your Father. Tell your Father how thankful you are for all you have, all you are and all that is around you. Bless him for all that He has given you and show Him your ATTITUDE OF GRATITUDE.

Today, on DAY 23 of our journey, we choose to open our eyes to all the things in our life and be grateful people who love God. We choose to recognize and express our gratitude every single day.

We choose not to be people who complain, whine or fail to see our blessings. We choose not be people who always see the negative, but to see positive in our circumstances. We choose to be people who bless others with our attitude of gratitude. Gratitude is contagious and today we choose to use it wisely to bless our Father and others around us.

Be blessed and be a blessing to others with your infectious smile, heart and words of gratitude. Bless God with your attitude of gratitude and be an example of a grateful life for all to witness.

SPEND 30 MINUTES IN MEDITATION, PRAYER AND READING HIS WORD. ASK GOD TO REVEAL TO YOU ALL OF THE BLESSINGS OF YOUR LIFE. WRITE THEM DOWN AND EXPRESS YOUR GRATITUDE.

(Watch the encouraging video at www.GodsAmazingPlans.com)

DAY 23: HAVE AN ATTITUDE OF GRATITUDE

LIST OUT THE 20 THINGS, THAT IF YOU WOKE UP TOMORROW AND THIS IS ALL YOU HAD, YOU WOULD BE GRATEFUL FOR:

_____
_____
_____
_____
_____
_____
_____
_____
_____
_____
_____
_____
_____
_____
_____
_____
_____
_____
_____

LIST OUT THE 20 THINGS, THAT IF YOU WOKE UP TOMORROW AND THIS IS ALL YOU HAD, YOU WOULD BE GRATEFUL FOR:

_____
_____
_____
_____
_____
_____
_____
_____
_____
_____
_____
_____
_____
_____
_____
_____
_____
_____
_____
_____
_____
_____
_____
_____
_____
_____
_____
_____
_____
_____
_____

LIST OUT THE 20 THINGS, THAT IF YOU WOKE UP TOMORROW AND THIS IS ALL YOU HAD, YOU WOULD BE GRATEFUL FOR:

_____
_____
_____
_____
_____
_____
_____
_____
_____
_____
_____
_____
_____
_____
_____
_____
_____
_____
_____
_____
_____
_____
_____
_____
_____
_____
_____
_____
_____
_____

LIST OUT THE 20 THINGS, THAT IF YOU WOKE UP TOMORROW AND THIS IS ALL YOU HAD, YOU WOULD BE GRATEFUL FOR:

_____
_____
_____
_____
_____
_____
_____
_____
_____
_____
_____
_____
_____
_____
_____
_____
_____
_____
_____
_____
_____
_____
_____
_____
_____
_____
_____
_____
_____
_____

DAY 24

WAIT UPON THE LORD'S TIMING

DAY 24: WAIT UPON THE LORD'S TIMING

Today is DAY 24 of our Challenge and today we are going to learn to WAIT UPON THE LORD'S TIMING. As hard as this can be, this is a very important component to faith and trusting that He has a great plan for you. We often think we are waiting and surrendering our desires, but really, we are not trusting wholeheartedly and confidently that He knows what He is doing, and that His timing is perfect. It's time to change that and learn to prayerfully wait upon the Lord's timing.

He tells us to ask, but we must believe. If we don't wait for His perfect timing, we are not trusting in His timing, or in His great plan. In fact, we are often trying to make it happen ourselves instead of waiting on the Lord's perfect timing. Wait for Him to unfold your plan. God is good, and His timing is perfect.

The first thing we need to understand about His timing is found in Psalm 18:30, *"God's timing is perfect, just as all of God's ways are perfect."* And in Habakkuk 2:3 we find one of my favorite verses, *"Faith in God also requires faith in His timing."*

In Galatians 4:4, we find *"God's timing is never early, and it's never been late."* In fact, from before our birth until the moment we take our last breath on Earth, our sovereign God is accomplishing His divine purposes in our lifetime. He is in complete control of everything and everyone from everlasting to everlasting. No event in history has put so much as a wrinkle in the timing of God's eternal plan, which He designed before the foundation of the world. Today we will learn to wait for God's perfect timing

Patience is a spiritual fruit found in Galatians 5:22. Scripture makes it clear that God is pleased with us when we display the virtue of patience. In Psalm 37:7 we learn, *"Be still before the*

LORD and wait patiently for Him." In Lamentations 3:25 we learn, "For God is good to those who wait for Him."

I don't know about you, but I am getting the hint from God that the wait is worth it. I choose to trust in His timing for my life and I encourage you in today's Challenge to begin trusting in Him; learning to trust that every day, in every circumstance, that His timing is perfect.

Our patience can reveal to Him the degree of trust we have in His timing. Our ability to wait on the Lord is largely related to how much we trust Him. When we trust in God with all our heart, forgoing reliance on our own, often erroneous understanding of circumstances, He will indeed give us direction. Thank you, good and faithful Father, for your divine timing in our lives.

In Psalm 27:14 we read, "Wait on the Lord; be of good courage, and He shall strengthen your heart; Wait, I say, on the Lord!" In that strength, keep close to God and to your duty. Wait on the Lord by faith and prayer and a humble resignation to His will. Wait, I say, on the Lord.

Whatever you do, grow not remiss in your dependence upon God. Keep up your spirits during the greatest dangers and difficulties: Be of good courage, let your heart be fixed on trusting in God. Let your mind stay upon Him. Let none of these things move you. Those who wait upon the Lord have reason to be of good courage.

CHALLENGE: Today, on DAY 24 of our journey, we choose to WAIT UPON THE LORD'S TIMING. We choose to wait upon His direction for our lives. We choose to wait upon His timing for all the things we want to do, say, start, and quit. We choose to trust in His timing in all circumstances. We choose to not move forward without Him leading the way. We choose to trust in God and show the world of our love and confidence in waiting for the Lord and His perfect timing.

Be blessed today and be a blessing to others by showing them how God is working in your life when you wait upon His perfect timing. You are a witness and proof of His perfect timing.

SPEND 30 MINUTES IN MEDITATION, PRAYER AND READING HIS WORD. ASK GOD TO REVEAL TO YOU ALL AREAS OF YOUR LIFE WHERE YOU ARE JUMPING AHEAD AND NOT WAITING FOR HIS PERFECT TIMING. WRITE THEM DOWN.

(Watch the encouraging video at www.GodsAmazing Plans.com)

DAY 24: WAIT UPON THE LORD'S TIMING

LIST THE THINGS YOU ARE JUMPING AHEAD OF GOD:

_____
_____
_____
_____
_____
_____
_____
_____
_____
_____
_____
_____
_____
_____
_____
_____
_____
_____
_____

LIST THE THINGS YOU ARE JUMPING AHEAD OF GOD:

_____
_____
_____
_____
_____
_____
_____
_____
_____
_____
_____
_____
_____
_____
_____
_____
_____
_____
_____
_____
_____
_____
_____
_____
_____
_____
_____

LIST THE WAYS YOU CAN WAIT ON HIS TIMING AND WHAT YOU CAN DO INSTEAD:

_____

_____

_____

_____

_____

_____

_____

_____

_____

_____

_____

_____

_____

_____

_____

_____

_____

_____

_____

_____

_____

_____

_____

_____

_____

_____

_____

_____

LIST THE WAYS YOU CAN WAIT ON HIS TIMING AND WHAT YOU CAN DO INSTEAD:

_____

_____

_____

_____

_____

_____

_____

_____

_____

_____

_____

_____

_____

_____

_____

_____

_____

_____

_____

_____

_____

_____

_____

_____

_____

_____

_____

DAY 25

PRAISE
GOD'S
FAITHFULNESS

DAY 25: PRAISE GOD'S FAITHFULNESS

Today is DAY 25 of our Challenge and we are nearing the end of our journey together. Today, we are going to learn to PRAISE HIS FAITHFULNESS. Father God always delivers exactly what we need exactly at the time we need it. He is always faithful, and His love is enduring. As He is faithful to you, praise His name and exalt it highly. Shout to the earth and let them hear of your miracles, testimonies, and glimpses of God's faithfulness in your life.

In Lamentations 3:22-23 we learn, *"The steadfast love of the Lord never ceases; His mercies never come to an end; they are new every morning; great is your faithfulness."* His faithfulness is great and new every single morning. Praise your Father for His faithfulness to you. You are His precious child. He loves you. He adores you. He is so faithful and will remain faithful for eternity.

In Deuteronomy 7:9 we are reminded, *"Know therefore that the Lord your God is good, the faithful God who keeps covenant and steadfast love with those who love him and keep His commandments to a thousand generations,"* Praise you Father for your steadfast love and faithfulness.

In Hebrews 10:23, we learn not to waiver, for God is faithful to His promises, *"Let us hold fast the confession of our hope without wavering, for He who promised is faithful."* Thank you, Father, for your promises and your faithfulness.

And in 1 Corinthians 1:9, Paul reminds us, *"God is faithful, by whom you were called into the fellowship of His Son, Jesus Christ our Lord."* We are reminded from our own miracles and testimonies that God is faithful, and today, we are going to seek His faithfulness, so we can begin to proclaim His greatness and praise His faithfulness to all who can hear.

CHALLENGE: Today, spend time in prayer, meditation, and worship. Praise Him and seek Him for insight to all His faithful promises which He has given faithfully. As you are praising Him, write in your journal all the many prayers that have been answered, the many doors that have been opened for you to walk through, and the many blessings He has bestowed upon your life.

Don't forget to also seek, remember, and write down all the doors that God has closed for you too. His faithfulness does not always come in what we think we want, but rather what He knows is best for us. Learn to recognize the things that you didn't get which are a glimpse of His faithfulness, protecting you, defending you, guiding you on your amazing journey. Write it all down in your journal. This is evidence of God's faithfulness to you.

He is faithful, and He wants to remind you of all the things He has done for you. Write the evidence down so you can easily share His faithfulness with the world and those that need to be encouraged and to know your faithful Father. Praise His faithfulness! Your praise of faithfulness may give others a glimpse of God that they may need to see in a time of despair and hopelessness. Praise His faithfulness often and openly for all the world to see.

CHALLENGE: Today, on DAY 25 of the Challenge, we choose to live a life full of praise for our Heavenly Father's faithfulness. We choose to share His love and goodness in our lives with others that need hope. We choose to share the faithfulness of His miracles in our lives. We choose to give hope to others by praising God's faithfulness, so they too will know the truth about trusting in a good and faithful God. Praise Him with your entire soul.

Be blessed today and be a blessing to others as you share your testimony of God's faithfulness to you and to them. Share the good news with them and don't keep it a secret.

SPEND 30 MINUTES IN MEDITATION, PRAYER AND READING HIS WORD. ASK GOD TO REVEAL TO YOU ALL THE BLESSINGS HE HAS BESTOWED UPON YOUR LIFE. INCLUDE DOORS HE HAS BOTH OPENED AND CLOSED TO GUIDE YOU TOWARDS HIS AMAZING PLAN FOR YOUR LIFE. WRITE IT ALL DOWN.

(Watch the encouraging video at www.GodsAmazingPlans.com)

DAY 25: PRAISE GOD'S FAITHFULNESS

ANSWERED PRAYERS:

_____
_____
_____
_____
_____
_____
_____
_____
_____
_____
_____
_____
_____
_____
_____
_____
_____
_____
_____
_____
_____

ANSWERED PRAYERS:

OPENED DOORS: (Divine connections and opportunities)

CLOSED DOORS: (Divine protection and guidance)

DAY 26

WATCH EXPECTANTLY

DAY 26: WATCH EXPECTANTLY FOR GOD

Today is DAY 26 of our Challenge and today we are going to WATCH EXPECTANTLY FOR GOD. Today, we are going to look around and watch expectantly that God will provide direction, perform a miracle in our lives, or answer a prayer that has been lifted up and united with others.

Look around expectantly today in amazement as you see God working in the lives of His children. He is faithful, and He desires for us to know the goodness of His heart.

In Micah 7:7 He tells us, *"But as for me, I watch expectantly in hope for the Lord, I wait for God my Savior; my God will hear me."* Today, we are going to watch expectantly like Micah and know that as we watch for our God, our Savior, that He will hear us, and we will see Him working in our lives.

Psalms 5:3 reads, *"In the morning, LORD, you hear my voice; in the morning I lay my requests before you and wait expectantly."* Such great guidance from David as he encourages us to go before the Lord daily and lay our requests before the Lord, then watch expectantly. He says, "Wait!" But I take it a step further and say, wait, watch expectantly and make sure your eyes are open to witness His miracles.

No matter how big or how small, we must be waiting and watching expectantly for His miracles. So many people are missing God's small miracles in their lives every day and it is so important to have eyes to see His small miracles. If you want to see His big miracles, open your eyes to see Him. His presence is with us in all moments of our lives. When we can become people watching expectantly, we will be in awe of our loving Father. Our relationship with Him will grow deeper and deeper, because we start becoming inseparable from Him and His will for our lives.

In James 1:6-7, He instructs us about our prayers and requests, *"But when you ask, you must believe and not doubt, because the one who doubts is like a wave of the sea, blown and tossed by the wind. That person should not expect to receive anything from the Lord."*

In these verses, James reveals an essential ingredient for answered prayer. Though he is referring to a request for divine wisdom here, the basic principle he reveals in this passage can be applied to almost any petition we make to the Lord. The key word is "expect." James says that if we pray, but don't really expect God to answer us, we shouldn't be surprised if He doesn't.

Taking that a step further, the opposite is true. If we expect God to answer our prayers according to His will, we should watch expectantly and should not be surprised when He does.

The dictionary defines "expect" as: *to look forward to, anticipate, watch or look for, wait for, count upon, hope for; believe and trust.* These are many of the terms that the authors of the Bible use, especially in the Psalms. I thought it was interesting that the dictionary listed "to despair of" as the opposite of "expect." I have often felt that the antidote for fear and despair was expecting God to act on our behalf. Now I see it confirmed in a dictionary definition.

Let God be your antidote to fear and doubt by placing all your trust in Him and WATCH EXPECTANTLY for Him to hear your prayers and know your heart. God is waiting for you to trust Him.

CHALLENGE: Today we are going to go before our Abba Father and spend time in His presence reminiscing about our life. Pray, meditate and ask God your Father to reveal to you all the times He has given you a miracle in your life. Ask Him to reveal them to you no matter how big or how small. Write them all down in your journal. Then, dig a little deeper with Him and ask Him to reveal to you the things you have previously never been aware of as a miracle from Him in your life. Then in prayer wait and watch expectantly to see if He shows you or shares supernatural miracles in your life that you were unaware of or missed seeing. Ask Him and then wait expectantly that He will speak to you.

Watch expectantly because His power and Spirit can, and will, speak to you about things of which you are completely unaware or oblivious to. Write those in the journal too. Pray over both miracles, seen and unseen, and ask Him to start from this day forward to give you the supernatural strength, courage, trust and faith to watch expectantly every day for His presence and His miracles.

Today, on DAY 26 of our journey, we choose to watch expectantly for God to show up in our lives. We choose to know that He hears us. We to choose to know that He sees us. And we choose to wait expectantly for answers to our prayers. We choose to wait upon His perfect timing and we will watch expectantly because we know our Father and our Father knows us.

Be blessed today and be a blessing to others by encouraging them to watch expectantly for God to do amazing things in their lives as they are witnessing you watch expectantly for Him too.

SPEND 30 MINUTES IN MEDITATION, PRAYER AND READING HIS WORD. ASK GOD TO REVEAL TO YOU ALL OF THE MIRACLES YOU HAVE SEEN IN YOUR LIFE. INCLUDE EVEN THE ONES YOU HAVE MISSED BUT NOW SEE SUPER-NATURALLY THROUGH YOUR FATHER'S EYES. LIST THEM ALL OUT IN YOUR JOURNAL.

(Watch the encouraging video at www.GodsAmazingPlans.com)

DAY 26: WATCH EXPECTANTLY

MIRACLES I'VE SEEN IN MY LIFE:

_____
_____
_____
_____
_____
_____
_____
_____
_____
_____
_____
_____
_____
_____
_____
_____
_____
_____
_____
_____
_____
_____
_____
_____
_____
_____
_____
_____
_____
_____
_____

MIRACLES I'VE SEEN IN MY LIFE:

MIRACLES UNSEEN BUT REVEALED TO ME TODAY:

DAY 27

RECOGNIZE GOD'S PLANS UNFOLDING

DAY 27: RECOGNIZE GOD'S PLANS UNFOLDING

Today is DAY 27 of our Challenge, and today, we are going to learn to RECOGNIZE GOD'S PLANS UNFOLDING. The first step to recognition is to search, to look, or to see. The definition of "recognize" is the identification in appearance or acknowledgement of existence or validity. God wants us to recognize His plans. He desires us to come to Him and to seek Him for every move along His amazing path and life for us.

Isaiah 30:21 says, *"And your ears shall hear a word behind you, saying, 'This is the way, walk in it,' when you turn to the right or when you turn to the left."*

He wants us to be aware of His Spirit always. If we want God to lead us to our destiny, but we cannot recognize Him unfolding the plans, how are we going to follow Him? We must learn to listen to Him with our ears like Isaiah. Then listen with our hearts and be fiercely obedient. This is how God's plan begins unfolding.

Today's Challenge is about learning to watch and recognize His plans unfolding around us in deed, action and events. The way to tap into this supernatural recognition is found in John 14:26, where John tells us, *"But the Helper, the Holy Spirit, whom the Father will send in my name, He will teach you all things and bring to your remembrance all that I have said to you."* It is through the power of God's Holy Ghost and Spirit that we will begin to have eyes to see Him. Ask Him to baptize you with His Holy fire so you can receive the gifts of the Spirit.

It is His Spirit that will give us ears to hear Him speak so clearly to us like Isaiah. It is He who will give us courage like David. It is He who will give us dreams of our future like Joseph. It is He who will give us faith like Job through trials and challenges along our journey. It is only the Holy Spirit and the power anointed in us that will help us learn to recognize His plans for our life as they begin to unfold.

We do not seek the world's approval or guidance to confirm or direct our paths; rather we seek our Father's Spirit to help us recognize Him and His amazing plans for our lives. Matthew 6:33 confirms, *"But seek first the kingdom of God and his righteousness, and all these things will be added to you."*

There is no question about it or any other way around it. Seek Him first and the steps to His amazing plans for your life will be clearly laid out for you to see. Only then will you begin to recognize His plans unfolding. Let your confirmation be found in Ephesians 1:19, *"And what is the immeasurable greatness of His power toward us who believe, according to the working of His great might."*

Through this journey, we have learned truth from lies, knowing your Father's voice from all others, learning to trust wholeheartedly, to surrender your will for His will, to wait patiently for the Lord's timing, to praise His faithfulness and to watch for Him expectantly.

All these lessons have taught us and prepared us to start looking around us and to recognize His plans unfolding. If you are not looking, it is hard to see and recognize. You must be coherent to His amazing plans and all the amazing details of perfection and preparation. If you are not looking expectantly, you can easily miss the subtle, but important signs, wonders and directions of your Father. His wondrous workmanship is unfolding all around us. He is building His plan for you. Look, watch, and stay alert to His presence and power in your life.

As you look around today, see if you can recognize His presence and obstacles being removed out of the path of your amazing plan. You must be looking, or you will miss them. The signs and wonders are all around us, but we must become aware and coherent to recognize them.

CHALLENGE: Today spend time in worship and prayer. Ask your Father to reveal to you the unfolding of His amazing plans. Ask Him to reveal to you circumstances, people, and events that have happened, or visions of things to come.

Ask Him to make you alert to His presence and divine movements along your path to His amazing plan. Then make a note of all the things He shared with you and pray over them. Pray over them often and watch your amazing plans begin to unfold.

Ask Him to continue to reveal more things to you, to open more doors and opportunities of these things for you. Write them all down in your journal as evidence that He has spoken to you. Then ask God to give you the courage and boldness to share this with someone. Write it, speak it, and acknowledge it to someone out lout so that God knows you heard Him, and more importantly, that you RECOGNIZE HIS PLANS UNFOLDING. This is not just a task for today's challenge, but I encourage you to make it a practice of your encounters and conversations with Jesus every day.

So today, on DAY 27 of our journey, we choose to spend time with our Abba Father. We choose to listen intently for Him to reveal His amazing plans to us. We choose to recognize His master plan. We choose to be alert and be coherent to God's presence in our lives. We choose to acknowledge God's power through His divine connections and timing. We choose to know that all things work together for our good when we love the Lord. Each step leads to your destiny and opens up the blessings of Heaven to drench you with God's great favor.

We must choose to recognize the small things, the seemingly insignificant things to others, and every step of the amazing plan

God is laying out for us.

Be blessed today and be a blessing to others as you share with them how God has a plan for each of us and you are recognizing your plans unfolding in your own life.

SPEND 30 MINUTES IN MEDITATION, PRAYER AND READING HIS WORD. THEN LIST ALL THE CONCRETE DETAILS YOU HEAR AND RECOGNIZE ABOUT YOUR AMAZING PLANS. WRITE EVERY DETAIL GOD REVEALS TO YOU.

(Watch the encouraging video at www.GodsAmazingPlans.com)

DAY 27: RECOGNIZE GOD'S PLANS UNFOLDING

THESE ARE MY AMAZING PLANS UNFOLDING BY MY FATHER:

_____
_____
_____
_____
_____
_____
_____
_____
_____
_____
_____
_____
_____
_____
_____
_____
_____
_____

THESE ARE MY AMAZING PLANS UNFOLDING BY MY FATHER:

_____
_____
_____
_____
_____
_____
_____
_____
_____
_____
_____
_____
_____
_____
_____
_____
_____
_____
_____
_____
_____
_____
_____
_____
_____
_____
_____
_____
_____
_____
_____
_____

THESE ARE MY AMAZING PLANS UNFOLDING BY MY FATHER:

_____
_____
_____
_____
_____
_____
_____
_____
_____
_____
_____
_____
_____
_____
_____
_____
_____
_____
_____
_____
_____
_____
_____
_____
_____
_____
_____
_____
_____
_____

DAY 28

LISTEN INTENTLY FOR GOD'S SPIRIT

DAY 28: LISTEN INTENTLY FOR GOD'S SPIRIT

Today is DAY 28 of our Challenge, and today, we are going to learn to LISTEN INTENTLY FOR GOD'S SPIRIT. Listening for earthly voices requires ears but listening to God's Spirit requires a surrendered and open heart. Matthew 7:7 tells us, *"Ask, and you shall receive. Seek, and you shall find. Knock, and it will be opened to you."*

The word "seek" means *to go in search of; to take pains to find; to strive for.* So how do you go in search of the Holy Spirit? You do this by spending quality time each day in private meditation seeking your Father's love and presence. This meditation is spent intently listening for the Holy Spirit, without any outside distractions. You must learn how to listen for His Spirit as we did on Day 6 "Learn Your Father's Voice."

You must learn how to let the Holy Spirit do the prompting (talking). You must learn that it is not books or friends, but the Holy Spirit, who gives us the gift of knowledge, the gift of discernment and the gift of prophesy to help answer our problems and give us His personal insight to things and choices around us.

In Jeremiah 33:3, He tells us, *"Call to me and I will answer you and tell you great, and unsearchable, things you do not know."* Wow, did you hear that? We can learn unsearchable things from God when we listen intently.

In Matthew 7:24, we get instructions, *"Therefore everyone who hears these words of mine and puts them into practice is like a wise man who built his house on the rock."* We must listen intently before we build, and we must hear Him before we can listen to Him.

In Mark 4:24, we are given more instruction with a promise, *"Consider carefully what you hear."* He continues, *"With the measure you use, it will be measured to you—and even more."* This is how God's amazing plan for us begins to grow. When we hear Him, and we become fiercely obedient to His will, He will continue to give us more details and insight

246

to His plans for our lives. The Spirit of God is speaking to the church. His words are so clear; but we must take the time to listen and quiet the clutter of our lives.

1 John 4:5 says, *"They are of the world. That is why they speak from the world's perspective, and the world listens to them. We are from God. Whoever knows God listens to us; whoever is not from God does not listen to us. That is how we know the Spirit of truth and the spirit of deception."* We are from God and created to know Spirit of truth from our Creator and master builder and know the difference between truth and deception of this world. We were created to listen to God.

We need to put aside our agendas, our routines, what we think we must do to get His attention and stop long enough to listen intently for His Spirit. In 1 Kings 19:12, we learn it is a small, still voice, *"And after the earthquake, a fire, but the Lord was not in the fire; and after the fire, a still small voice."* To hear a still small voice, we must intentionally be quiet and listen. We must learn to be still in His presence and listen.

Today on DAY 28 of our Challenge we choose to LISTEN INTENTLY FOR GOD'S SPIRIT. We choose to take His words and let them penetrate our hearts, giving us wisdom and understanding, to live out His amazing plans.

In James 1:19 we learn, *"My dear brothers and sisters, take note of this: Everyone should be quick to listen, slow to speak and slow to become angry."* This doesn't only mean quick to listen to others in conversation, but also to be quick to listen to God's Spirit, even in dispute, in conflict, or in important decisions, so we can hear our Father's love and respond like Jesus.

Today, sit in His presence and listen for His Spirit through the heat of His fire, the breeze of a Spirt filled wind, the peace that surpasses all understanding, or through the love of another human being. He is speaking to us. As we learn to adjust our spiritual listening devices we can hear Him. We were designed to hear His voice and His Spirit.

CHALLENGE: Listen intently today for His Spirit to speak to you and guide you. As you pray, ask Him to speak to you about these four C's of listening skills and how to improve these skills to listen to Him more effectively and respond accordingly.

The four C's of listening better and learning more.

Pray about these skills:

1. COMMUNICATION (better listening skills to hear Him clearly).
2. COMPREHENSION (to understand His plan and His immense love for you).
3. CONFIDENCE (trusting Him wholeheartedly and being fiercely obedient to Him).
4. CHANGE (transformation into the person He created you to be).

Then, whatever wisdom He tells you, write it down. Write it all down. Keep writing as He speaks to you and shares with you His secrets to life and living the abundant life that He has promised you.

Today, on DAY 28 of our journey, we choose to seek God as we are confident we will find Him. We choose to listen intently for His Spirit. We choose to listen for His still, small voice, to learn truth from deception. We choose to build our lives upon the rock of Jesus Christ. We choose to find quiet time to spend with Him because we desire to know His heart and His plans for us. We choose to surrender and listen intently with our hearts wide open. We choose Jesus as our counselor and we choose to trust His loving voice and wise counsel.

Be blessed today and be a blessing to others by listening intently to them and to God's still, small voice, as He directs your every word and step. Bless them by sharing what you hear from your Father.

SPEND 30 MINUTES IN MEDITATION, PRAYER AND READING GOD'S WORD. ASK GOD TO REVEAL TO YOU THE WAYS IN WHICH YOU CAN DEVELOP AND INCREASE YOUR LISTENING SKILLS AS LISTED BELOW. WRITE EVERY DETAIL HE

REVEALS TO YOU ABOUT EACH SKILL. PRAY OVER THEM FREQUENTLY.

(Watch the encouraging video at www.GodsAmazingPlans.com)

DAY 28: LISTEN INTENTLY FOR GOD'S SPIRIT

WRITE WHAT JESUS TELLS YOU ABOUT THE FOLLOWING FOUR C'S.

COMMUNICATION (better listening skills to hear Him clearly):

_____
_____
_____
_____
_____
_____
_____
_____
_____
_____
_____
_____
_____
_____
_____
_____
_____
_____
_____
_____

COMPREHENSION (to understand His plan and His immense love for you):_____
_____

COMPREHENSION (to understand His plan and His immense love for you):_____

_____
_____
_____
_____
_____
_____
_____
_____
_____
_____
_____
_____
_____
_____
_____
_____
_____
_____
_____

CONFIDENCE (to understand His plan and His immense love for you):_____

_____
_____
_____
_____
_____
_____
_____
_____
_____
_____
_____
_____
_____

CONFIDENCE (to understand His plan and His immense love for you):_____

_____
_____
_____
_____
_____
_____
_____
_____
_____

CHANGE (transformation into the person He created you to be):_____

_____
_____
_____
_____
_____
_____
_____
_____
_____
_____
_____
_____
_____
_____
_____
_____
_____
_____
_____

DAY 29

ENJOY

GOD'S

PRESENCE

DAY 29: ENJOY GOD'S PRESENCE

Today is DAY 29 of the Challenge and we are going to ENJOY OUR FATHER'S PRESENCE. Psalm 16:11 tells us, *"You make known to me the path of life; in your presence there is fullness of joy; at your right hand are pleasures forevermore."*

And in Acts 3:20-21 we find our restoration, *"That times of refreshing may come from the presence of the Lord."* Today we are going to seek His refreshment and fullness of joy as we are in His presence.

Today, laugh, love and live in His presence. God gave Adam and Eve a beautiful Garden of Eden to enjoy and today we will return to experience it as God intended and designed it for us to enjoy.

The Bible reveals in 1 Corinthians 14:33, *"God is not the author of confusion, but of peace."* Perfect peace, order, and innocence characterized life in the beginning for the first humans because they were initially only influenced by God; and for a brief time, they obeyed Him. His presence was still there but disobedience separated them for a time from Him as they sinned, felt ashamed and then hid from Him.

Today we are going to reflect on the Garden of Eden from the beginning and seek His presence to understand how He intended for us to live life under His provision, guidance and love for us. We are going to learn to be influenced only by God and fight all temptation of being influenced by others and deceived by the enemy.

In Genesis 2:8, we are introduced to the location where our first parents were placed by God, *"God planted a garden for the first humans to learn, live, develop and work in."* The name of this location—Eden—provides a description of what it was like. Eden means "pleasure" or "paradise." While we can't go back to this land of pleasure and paradise, we can restore and refresh ourselves daily in experiencing God's presence as it was in His first creation.

We are going to learn to enjoy our Father's presence and recognize that our time with our Father isn't just for help, but also for pleasure and to experience joy and happiness. Let us celebrate our relationship with Him and learn to enjoy Him as a confidant, advisor and best friend.

This garden represented perfect peace and safety for the first human beings. There was no danger, no worry, no violence, no sickness and no stress. Why was life so idyllic and perfect in the Garden of Eden? The answer is because God's presence was there, and sin had not yet entered the human realm. Again, while we can't go back to the Garden of Eden, we can begin to learn and understand God's intention for His chosen people. And if we surrender our lives and desires to be in sync with His, we can live in this world as close to the pleasure and paradise of what God intended for us in the beginning.

Of course, we face the desires of flesh, and the temptations and pains of this world, but that is when we most need to seek our Heavenly Father for truth, comfort, direction, forgiveness, grace, and mercy. His presence can refresh us. In Zephaniah 3:17 we learn, *"The Lord your God is in your midst, a mighty one who will save; He will rejoice over you with gladness; He will quiet you by His love; He will exult over you with loud singing."* So, when you need Him, go and enjoy His presence!

CHALLENGE: Today, spend time in prayer, worship and meditation. Learn to laugh, love, and live in His presence. Matthew 5:8 says, *"Blessed are the pure in heart, for they shall see God."*

Today, go see God. Visit Him and enjoy His presence. In Isaiah 60:1, He tells us, *"Arise, shine, for your light has come and the glory of the Lord has risen upon you."* Go be with God and enjoy your time with Him. You can experience His presence when you seek Him.

God gave Adam and Eve a beautiful Garden of Eden to enjoy with everything their hearts could desire. He has given us the same opportunity to enjoy Him when we seek Him and enter His presence. Do not eat of the spoiled and rotten fruit with which the enemy will tempt you. Enjoy His presence and ask Him to always be present as your best friend. Today, worship and rejoice in His presence. Call upon

Him to spend intimate time with you, to uncover the mysteries of His love and amazing plans for you.

After you pray and spend time in His presence, write down all the things He revealed to you. Perhaps His original plans for your life, or the joy He wants you to experience in life; or perhaps He tells you to rest more, laugh more, play more, or to give up things that are bogging you down and creating unnecessary pain in your life. Write it all down!

These conversations are God's wisdom spoken directly to you. Read them every day and reflect on His counsel to you. These are the intimate conversations with your Father, where your peace and rest come to life. These are the conversations that will lead your steps along His amazing plan for your life and keep you in sync with His will. ENJOY GOD'S PRESENCE.

Today, on DAY 29 of our journey, we choose to enjoy God's presence. We choose to spend time relaxing and playing in His presence. We choose to reflect on what is good, and God's original plan for His chosen children. We choose to seek Him. We choose to obey Him. We choose to dedicate our lives to making Him our priority. We choose to surrender to Him as our Lord and Savior. We choose to love like Jesus and be Jesus like to this world.

Be blessed today and be a blessing to others as you enjoy the presence of the Lord and soak up His love for you. Share His love with others today and every day as you teach them to enjoy God's presence.

SPEND 30 MINUTES IN GOD'S PRESENCE THROUGH MEDITATION, PRAYER AND READING HIS WORD. AS YOU IMAGINE THE ORDER AND PERFECTION OF THE GARDEN OF EDEN. CONSIDER WHAT GOODNESS GOD WANTS FOR YOUR LIFE. WHAT DID GOD REVEAL TO YOU? WRITE IT ALL DOWN.

(Watch the encouraging video at www.GodsAmazingPlans.com)

DAY 29: ENJOY GOD'S PRESENCE

WHAT GOODNESS DOES GOD WANT IN YOUR LIFE?

FATHER, IN YOUR PRESENCE I LEARN:

WHAT GOODNESS DOES GOD WANT IN YOUR LIFE?

FATHER, IN YOUR PRESENCE I LEARN:

WHAT GOODNESS DOES GOD WANT IN YOUR LIFE?

FATHER, IN YOUR PRESENCE I LEARN:

DAY 30

PRAISE

GOD'S

NAME

DAY 30: PRAISE GOD'S NAME

Today is DAY 30 of our 30-Day Challenge. Congratulations, you did it! I pray that you were blessed through this 30-day journey and that your life has been impacted in some dramatic way through Jesus Christ himself. I pray that He has drawn you closer to Him, that you have heard His voice more clearly, that you have been directed to a new destination and encountered your next steps to living out your amazing plan.

Today, on DAY 30, we are going to PRAISE GOD'S NAME. We are going to praise His name all day long. In Psalm 150:1-6, we read, *"Praise the Lord. Praise God in His sanctuary; praise Him in His mighty heavens. Praise Him for His acts of power; praise Him for His surpassing greatness. Praise Him with the sounding of the trumpet, praise Him with the harp and lyre, praise Him with timbral and dancing, praise Him with the strings and pipe, praise Him with the clash of cymbals, and praise Him with resounding cymbals. Let everything that has breath praise the Lord. Praise the Lord."*

Today, shout His name. Halleluiah! Hosanna! King of Kings! Lord of Lords! Alpha and Omega! Abba Father! Praise Him! Praise Him! Praise Him forever! For He is good and deserves our praises.

CHALLENGE: Today, spend time alone in quiet, and in a group, and praise His name. Speak it, write it, shout it, whisper it. Praise Him with your whole heart and let everyone know the loving God you serve and the amazing plan He has for your life. Let everyone know the amazing things He has already done for you.

Then write a letter to your Father giving Him thanks and praise for who He is, and what He has done for you. Praise Him and tell Him how much He means to you and how much you love Him.

Write it all down. Pour out your heart of praise and let it become a habit every day. Hebrews 13:15 tells us, *"Through Jesus, therefore, let us continually offer to God a sacrifice of praise—the fruit of lips that openly profess His name."* Let our praise be a continual offering to our Abba Father for His love and sacrifice.

Today, on DAY 30, the final day of the Challenge, we choose to PRAISE GOD'S NAME. We choose to glorify Him with our words and actions. We choose to glorify Him, giving Him all the honor and all the glory for all the good things that have happened, and we know will happen in our life. We choose to tell everybody we know about who God is and how much He loves us. We choose to praise His name in good times and we choose to praise His name in difficult times. We choose from this day forward, to commit time to God every day and praise His name.

Be blessed today and every day and be a blessing to others by sharing this 30-Day Challenge to living out God's Amazing Plans in their lives. Bless others so they may experience the greatness and fullness of God in their lives and begin to search out God's amazing plans for their own lives.

PRAY, MEDITATE AND GO BEFORE YOUR FATHER TO PRAISE HIM AS YOU REMEMBER ALL THE THINGS GOD HAS DONE FOR YOU. WRITE IT ALL DOWN AND READ IT OFTEN. PRAISE GOD'S NAME.

(Watch the encouraging video at www.GodsAmazingPlans.com)

DAY 30: PRAISE GOD'S NAME.

DEAR ABBA FATHER, MY KING, MY SOURCE OF ALL POWER, I PRAISE YOUR NAME:

_____
_____
_____
_____

DEAR ABBA FATHER, MY KING, MY SOURCE OF ALL POWER, I PRAISE YOUR NAME:

DEAR ABBA FATHER, MY KING, MY SOURCE OF ALL POWER, I PRAISE YOUR NAME:

_____
_____
_____
_____
_____
_____
_____
_____
_____
_____
_____
_____
_____
_____
_____
_____
_____
_____
_____
_____
_____
_____
_____
_____
_____
_____
_____
_____
_____
_____
_____
_____

DEAR ABBA FATHER, MY KING, MY SOURCE OF ALL POWER, I PRAISE YOUR NAME:

_____

_____

_____

_____

_____

_____

_____

_____

_____

_____

_____

_____

_____

_____

_____

_____

_____

_____

_____

_____

_____

_____

_____

_____

_____

_____

_____

_____

_____

_____

_____

LIVE THE ABUNDANT LIFE

SHARE YOUR STORY, REVELATIONS AND AMAZING PLANS

WITH US

www.GodsAmazingPlans.com

ENCOURAGEMENT TO CONTINUE DAILY TIME WITH JESUS

Thank you for joining us on this 30-Day Challenge to live out YOUR amazing plan. We pray you heard the voice of God clearly and listened intently to the direction He is calling you to walk so that you will become fiercely obedient to His will.

I encourage you to repeat this Challenge as often as you can to develop the skills in this book and these 30 key principles God revealed to me in my life. Repeating this Challenge will also help you continue to commit time daily with your Heavenly Father in prayer, worship, meditation, conversation and reading His words in the Holy Bible.

If you are a ministry leader, I encourage you to share this 30-Day Challenge with your bible study, church, small group or accountability group and help facilitate their journey through it. You will be a blessing and instrumental in helping create discipline for them to become a faithful follower of Jesus Christ and live out their amazing plans.

If you are not a leader, but feel God calling you to create a small life group or accountability group, I strongly encourage you to be obedient and see how God will use you to facilitate this 30-Day Challenge with them. If you need help, we would be happy to help guide you.

I would love to hear your stories and encounters with Jesus through your journey and in the lives of those you continue this journey with over another 30 days. Please contact us for any questions, comments or assistance at **www.GodsAmazingPlans.com.**

If you would like to have Tamara speak with your ministry or share her testimony on this book or any topic in this book, please contact her at TamaraDoss@GodsAmazingPlans.com or GodsAmazingPlans.com

AMAZING LIFE MINISTRIES BELIEFS AND VALUES

Amazing Life Ministries believes in God the Father, Jesus Christ the son and the Holy Spirit.

We believe in the Crucifixion and that Jesus sacrificed His life in exchange for ours. We believe in the resurrection and that Jesus rose again on the third day and that He is sitting at the right hand of His Father. Be believe that Jesus died to forgive us of our sins and provide a way for our salvation and to live eternally in Heaven alongside our Heavenly Father.

We believe that God so loved the world that He gave His one and only Son that whoever believes in Him shall not die but have everlasting life. We believe in Confession, Repentance and Restoration through God's great love and power.

We believe in the Holy Spirit and He was sent to live in us and with us here on earth and be the source for our intimate and direct communication through Jesus Christ to our Father. We believe that the Holy Spirit was sent as our Guide, Healer, Counselor and source of Truth. We believe that Jesus Christ has anointed us with the power to forgive, love, heal, defend and live out His amazing plan for our lives.

Our primary mission at Amazing Life Ministries is to help people to recognize, embrace and live out God's Amazing Plans. We are founded on 1 Corinthians 2:9 and believe that the abundant life is for everyone.

Reggie and Tamara Doss, Founders of Amazing Life Ministries

To learn more About Tamara Doss, Amazing Life Ministries and God's Amazing Plans radio show, please visit:
www.GodsAmazingPlans.com

ABOUT THE AUTHOR

Tamara is busy with her three adopted sons as they are all active in sports and school. Tamara grew up in Greeley, Colorado and attended University of Northern Colorado where she studied Business and Marketing. Tamara has 30 years of experience in marketing and business management. She has exceled in her professional career as a business owner and Executive Sales Professional and is innovative, progressive and desires to see people achieve their best and break new ground in their personal and professional lives. She is passionate about helping others live the abundant life Jesus promises them.

She is a Christian blogger and author of several books to inspire and encourage others to see glimpses of God's purpose and greatness in their lives. She is also a Radio Host of **God's Amazing Plans** on www.HopeRadio247.com Fridays at 10:00am to 12:00pm PST.

The Doss family has a ministry called **Amazing Life Ministries** which focuses on helping others to recognize, embrace and live out **God's Amazing Plans** in their own lives and to experience God's glory in His fullness. Amazing Life Ministries' is founded on bible verse 1 Corinthians 2:9 *"No eye can see, no ear can hear, no mind can conceive of the greatness in store for those who love the Lord"* and theme song is "Floating" by her dear friend Esther Rose Neal, worship leader and musician.

Tamara desires to share her love for God to all people, male and female, young and old. She knows that the secret to life is embracing the truth of Jesus Christ and His love for us.

Her other favorite bible verses are Jeremiah 29:11 *"For I know the plans I have for you"* declares the Lord *"plans to prosper you and not to harm you, plans to give you hope and a future"* and Romans 8:28 *"All things work for good for those that love the Lord and are called according to His purpose."*

BE BLESSED
AND
BE A
BLESSING
TO
OTHERS